GUNS FOR SALE

Guns for Sale

War and Capitalism
in English Literature, 1851–1939

by Ivan Melada

Jefferson and London McFarland, 1983

Library of Congress Cataloguing-in-Publication Data

Melada, Ivan.
    Guns for sale.

    Bibliography: p.
    Includes index.
    1. War and literature. 2. English literature — 19th
century — History and criticism. 3. English literature —
20th century — History and criticism. 4. Capitalism and
literature. 5. Politics and literature. I. Title.
II. Title: War and capitalism.
PR468.W37M44 1983   820'.9'358   83-42893

ISBN 0-89950-079-X

Manufactured in the United States of America

McFarland & Company, Inc., Publishers
    Box 611, Jefferson, North Carolina 28640

To my wife Dale Leavesley Melada
and to the memory of her great-uncle
Joe Moroge who died on the
Western Front in 1918

Contents

Acknowledgments

I wish to thank the Research Allocations Committee of the University of New Mexico for underwriting three summer trips to the Huntington Library where I was able to read widely in the eighty-year period covered in this study. I am also grateful to the Regents of the University of New Mexico for granting me a semester's sabbatical leave during which I assembled my material and wrote the book. Members of the staff of the Huntington were particularly kind. Mary Wright of the Rare Book Room patiently recorded the scores of titles which I requested. Besides being superbly creative in finding housing for Huntington readers, Noelle Jackson of Reader Services typed the final manuscript.

I also want to thank the editors who graciously permitted me to use material which I had published earlier in their journals. With varying degrees of alteration, the following chapters had originally appeared as articles:

Chapter Three: "Ars Vincit Omnia" as "John Ruskin's Ambivalence Toward War." *Études Anglaises*, 32 (1979), 294–302.

Chapter Four: "The Treasurer of the Eastern Question Association" as "William Morris's Entry into Public Life." *Studies in the Humanities*, 8 (1980), 38–40.

Chapter Five: "Dr. Strangelove, circa 1899" as "George Gissing's 'Anti-Jingo Book': *The Crown of Life* and the 'Question of Peace'." *Gissing Newsletter*, 14 (1978), 3 – 18.

Chapter Eight: "Men Who Marched Away" as "The Politics of Writers in the Trenches." *Dalhousie Review*, 59 (1979), 338–349.

Chapters Nine: "Able Journalism, Sob-Brotherly and Sane"
and Ten: "Agents, Assassins, and Armaments" expand-
ed from "Graham Greene and the Munitions Makers:
the Historical Context of *A Gun for Sale*." *Studies in the
Novel*, 13 (1981), 303–321.

Finally, I am deeply grateful to my wife Dale for her support,
encouragement, and patience.

"We must face the unpleasant
truths that normal life today is a life
in factories and offices, that even
war has evolved from an adventure
into a business, that even farming
has become scientific, that insurance
has taken the place of charity, that
status has given way to contract."

E.M. Forster
Two Cheers for Democracy

Preface

This study grew out of a contemplation of Shelley's announce-
ment that poets are the unacknowledged legislators of the world.
In recent times poets have had not a few occasions to address themselves to both the governors and the governed as Shelley had in
"The Masque of Anarchy" and "Song to the Men of England." But
Shelley is an anomaly when one thinks of other less conspicuously
political but major literary figures of the nineteenth and twentieth
centuries. The question to be asked, then, is what moves the man of
letters to become conspicuous and legislate for mankind? What sort
of ethical issue will prompt him to raise his voice in comment or
protest?

The problem of modern war is that sort of issue. We have had
a hundred and fifty years of "modern" little wars and great wars,
brushfires and holocausts. The concept of warfare has altered fun-
damentally since the Napoleonic era just as art and science have
taken new directions since that time. After Napoleon and Clausewitz, war could no longer be considered the sport of dynasties, en-
gaged in by small professional armies maneuvering on the chess-
board of land and sea, preferring, as good chess form dictates, to
checkmate by strategy rather than win by attrition. The small professional armies of the pre-Napoleonic era have given way to the
concept of the nation in arms: regular army volunteers supported
by large reserves of conscripts. Dynastic quarrels once fought by
armies of uniformed retainers have thus become people's wars.
That poets have done more than merely sing of arms and the man
is only too obvious in the literature of the First World War.

1

Much has been written and said in the last decade about the paramount need for relevance in the education of the present generation. This study disclaims any intention of striving to fulfill that need. Instead, it seeks to reveal a continuity of concerns over the last century, concerns peculiar to modern industrial civilization. The vocabulary of the last decade has been useful, however. When we read Ruskin on art and war in the 1860's and 1870's, for example, there is hardly a better way of identifying his attitude than to say that he wants to rearrange "national priorities." The observation that a century is, after all, not such a long time is made with the illuminative power of an epiphany by John Fowles in *The French Lieutenant's Woman* when the narrator, equally at home in this century as in the last, comments upon the resemblance between a Victorian gentlewoman and her great-granddaughter. To paraphrase T.S. Eliot, we must be aware of both the pastness of the past and its presence.

Introduction

My preparations are defensive.
Your preparations are offensive.
I must prepare because you are preparing.
I am preparing because you prepare.
Then let us prepare.
We will still go on preparing.
                    —von Suttner, *Lay Down Your Arms*

If we look in the nineteenth century for the industrialist who
looms largest, history and fiction present us with the cotton manufacturer. In his autobiography Robert Owen testifies that the manufacture of cotton offered the best opportunities for the entrepreneur. The prominence of cotton men is underscored by the descriptive appellations that begin to appear in print. There are the "cotton
lords" and the "cottonocracy." In *Michael Armstrong* (1840), Mrs.
Trollope coins the word "millocrat," and Carlyle writes about the
"Millocracy" in *Past and Present* (1842). Despite the uncomplimen-
tary names, the cotton manufacturer remained an employer de-
voted to the arts of peace. But the Industrial Revolution and the
Machine Age also advanced the art of war. The Great Exhibition of
1851 celebrated England's preeminence as an industrial nation, and
Prince Albert was optimistic about that occasion's ushering in an era
of universal peace. At the same time, one of the exhibits at the
Crystal Palace was Krupp's new concept in artillery, the cast-steel
cannon. Twenty years later, improved models were destined to be
a decisive factor in the Franco-Prussian war and in Prussia's

undisguised pride in her military achievements. The rest is modern history.

It is what Shaw's cannon maker, Andrew Undershaft, rather than what Carlyle's cotton spinner, Plugson of Undershot, symbolizes that is the subject of this study. Prevalent in the 1930's was a feeling that wars were promoted by munitions makers. This study is an effort to trace the evolution of that feeling about the role of human agents in creating the conditions of war. It is above all an account of a changing awareness of the origins of war, a moving away from the centuries-old belief that dynasties made war for their own purposes to a modern, if equally simplistic, notion that capitalism's heavy industry covertly encouraged war for its own profit. That change in attitude begins to take shape in the mid-Victorian England of John Bright, becomes more sharply defined in the Edwardian Age and arrives at its fullest expression in the war *Geist* of Georgian England in the thirties.

One

"This Huckster Put Down War!"

I.

In the mid-nineteenth century Richard Cobden is a political figure closely associated with John Bright. Cobden is best remembered in the history books for his work in domestic policy as head of the Anti-Corn Law League. Together with Bright, he succeeded in convincing Sir Robert Peel of the need to eliminate the tax on bread. Peel responded with the repeal of the Corn Laws in 1846 and thereby removed the import restrictions on grain. Shortly after that, in his final speech to the Commons, he praised Cobden as the man responsible for the success of that measure.[1*] Domestic commercial policy was not the only interest of Richard Cobden who was to be called "the International Man."[2] A few years later he took an active part in allaying the fear of French invasion which disturbed England for fifteen years after the Revolution of 1848.

As a mid-century advocate of peace and disarmament, Cobden made three observations about the nature of modern war which history subsequently has confirmed. For one, he reminded his countrymen that war scares are often promoted by those who for various reasons are not in a state of panic themselves. Secondly, he recognized that henceforth arms technology would be as highly regarded as generalship as a decisive agent in battle. Finally, he saw the considerable demand on a nation's resources that modern technological warfare would make.

See Chapter Notes, beginning on page 115.

In *The Three Panics* (1862), Cobden analyzes the fears of invasion from France that alarmed the English in 1847–1848, again in 1851–1853, and once more in 1859–1861. He scorns the arguments of English "Invasionists" who were persuaded or were persuading Englishmen that the French were on the way. Laying aside French statements and examining only English official accounts, Cobden concludes "…that, as a nation, we have borne false witness against our neighbours: that, without a shadow of a doubt, we have accused them, repeatedly, during a long series of years, of meditating an unprovoked attack on our shores, in violation of every principle of international law and in contempt of all the obligations of morality and honour."[3] That accusation is an insult to the intelligence and the honor of France. To harbor suspicions of France secretly preparing for a naval war with England is to regard the French as having the minds of children. The French know that they could not single-handedly contest England's supremacy at sea, "…and this is not so much owing to our superiority in government arsenals — where notorious mismanagement countervails our advantages — as to the vast and unrivalled resources we possess in private establishments for the construction of ships and steam machinery."[4] In casting about for who is to blame, Cobden does not name special interests so much as he lists motives: "In inquiring into the origin of these panics, it would be folly to conceal from ourselves that they have been sometimes promoted by those who have not themselves shared in the delusion. Personal rancour, professional objects, dynastic aims, the interests of party, and other motives, may have played a large part."[5] Instead of singling out individuals Cobden lodges a general complaint against political parties in office for abetting the "Invasionists" by stepping up armaments: "But successive governments have rendered themselves wholly responsible for the invasion panics, by making them the plea for repeated augmentations of our armaments. It is this which has impressed the public mind with a sense of danger and which has drawn the youth of the middle class from civil pursuits, to enrol themseles for military exercises — a movement not the less patriotic because it originated in groundless apprehensions."[6] What can be done about alarmists and for the people they incite to panic over possible foreign invasions? In his reply to that question, Cobden reveals a mutual regard for that "most cautious and sagacious of our statesmen," Sir Robert Peel, by recommending a speech of Peel's made in 1850 at the end of his career: "I believe that, in time of peace, we must by our retrenchment, *consent to incur some risk.* I venture to say that, if you choose to have all the garrisons of all your colonial possessions in a complete state, and to have all your fortifications secure against attack, no amount of annual expenditure will be sufficient to accomplish your object."[7]

It cannot be held that Cobden was capable of writing at great length in protest against the false alarms of war because he lacked the imagination of disaster. His courageous opposition to the "Invasionists" was not founded upon a blissful ignorance of the destructive capacity of mid-nineteenth century inventions for the military. In a pamphlet comparing the international climate of 1793 to that of 1853, he displayed both his knowledge of and his apprehensions about the advances that the men of the Machine Age had made in weapons:

> ...war itself, owing to the application of greater science to the process of human destruction has become a much more costly pursuit. So great has been the *improvement* in the construction of horizontal shells, and other contrivances in gunnery that even Sir Howard Douglas who could recount with the utmost complacency the capabilities of Congreve rockets, Shrapnell shells, grape, and canister, seems struck with compunction at the contemplation of this last triumph of his favourite science. But a still greater discovery has been since announced by Mr. Nasmyth, who offers to construct a monster mortar for maritime warfare, which shall lie snugly ensconsed in the prow of a bomb-proof floating steam vessel, and on being propelled against a ship of war, the concussion shall cause an explosion with force sufficient to tear a hole in her side "as big as a church door."[8]

Cobden was not convinced by the balance of terror argument that the more deadly the weaponry the more disinclined men would be to fight: "When crossbows were first brought into use, the clergy preached against them as murderous. Upon the introduction of the 'sight' to assist the eye in taking aim with cannon, on board ship, the old gunners turned their quids, looked sentimental and pronounced the thing no better than 'murder.' But war lost none of its attractions by such discoveries; it is at best but gambling for 'glory'; and whatever be the risk, men will always take the long odds against death."[9]

The skill and inventiveness of armaments engineers had become as indispensible in modern war as military leadership, resourcefulness, and daring had been in the past; but technology would cost: "For it is quite certain that the Nasmyths, Fairbairns and Stephensons would play quite as great a part as the Nelsons and Collingwoods, in any future wars; and we all know that to give full scope to their engineering powers involves an almost unlimited expenditure of capital."[10] Therein lay Cobden's belief in the possibility of a future without war. His optimism, which the last century has proved not a little naive, resided in the costliness of modern weapons as a deterrent. Not the fear of annihilation by monster guns but the price tag on those guns would make nations hesitate to make war an instrument of national policy: "But I have great hopes from the expensiveness of war, and the cost of preparation; and should war break out between two great nations, I have no doubt that the immense consumption of material, and the rapid destruction of property would have the effect of very soon bringing the combatants to reason, or exhausting their re- sources."[11]

II.

It was a similar conclusion about the economic burdens of war that made John Bright the object of Tennyson's scorn in *Maud*. Together with his humanitarian objections, Bright regarded the

"This Huckster Put Down War!"

Crimean War as a drain on national funds better spent at home. Throughout his public career, he opposed support of large standing armies and backed the principle of an extended free trade as the means of avoiding armed conflict. As for singling out a particular group as instigators, Bright was more explicit than Cobden in identifying war interests with money interests.

In a letter to Absalom Watkin written in 1854, Bright set out his humanitarian and moral arguments against a war which he considered criminal and not in the best interests of England. He describes the aftermath of battle, a rhetorical technique intended as an appeal to human sympathy in the literature of nineteenth century war protest (but one which Ford Madox Ford would later claim to be hopelessly ineffectual as a dissuasive):

> You have heard the tidings from the Crimea; you have, perhaps, shuddered at the slaughter; you remember the terrific picture — I speak not of the battle, and the charge, and the tumultuous excitement of the conflict, but of the field after the battle — Russians in their frenzy or their terror shooting Englishmen who would have offered them water to quench their agony of thirst; Englishmen, in crowds, rifling the pockets of the men they had slain or wounded, taking their few shillings or roubles, and discovering among the plunder of the stiffening corpses, images of the "Virgin and the child"....[12]

Those are the crimes and horrors into which a Christian government has heedlessly blundered. The populace may applaud such a course, but for Bright, unmoved by public sentiment, there are higher laws which supersede the English Constitution:

> You must excuse me if I cannot go with you. I will have no part in this terrible crime. My hands shall be unstained with the blood which is being shed. The necessity of maintaining themselves in office may influence an adminstration; delusions may mislead a people...but no respect for men who form a Government, no regard have I for "going with the stream," and no fear of being deemed wanting in patriotism, shall influence me in favour of a

policy which, in my conscience, I believe to be as criminal before God as it is destructive to the true interest of my country.[13]

Bright's evaluation of the officeholder's motive for going along might be shared, but what of the "delusions" in the minds of the English people? By far it was morbid fear of Russia that generated support for the war in England (a fear which later put Disraeli and England into a grotesque moral position at the time of the Eastern Question of 1876-1878). That anti-Russian sentiment and its timelessness are adequately revealed by a correspondent of Cobden's in 1855: "This, then, is my creed. I look upon Russia as the personification of Despotism—the apostle of Legitimacy. In the present state of Poland and Hungary we see her work.... Such a power can be curbed only by war, and must be curbed sooner or later, if Europe is to remain free.... If we believe that God wills the liberty and happiness of mankind, how can we doubt that we are doing God's work in fighting for liberty against aggression."[14]

By dissociating himself from the motives of his government and the mood of the people, Bright retreated into isolation but not silence. To the House of Commons he delivered his famous "angel of death" speech in 1855. The climax of his oratory was an appeal to all levels of society urging an end to the Crimean War: "The angel of death has been throughout the land; you may almost hear the beating of his wings. There is no one, as when the first-born were slain of old, to sprinkle with blood the lintel and the two sideposts of our doors, that he may spare and pass on; he takes his victims from the castle of the noble, the mansion of the wealthy, and the cottage of the poor and the lowly; and it is on behalf of all these classes that I make this solemn appeal."[15] Bright's compelling power as a speaker is owing both to his unassailable moral position sanctioned by higher laws and, as the angel of death paragraph shows, to the rhetorical artistry of his argument. The Old Testament allusion to the smiting of the first-born invites his auditors to share a common Christian past. The Angel of Death, vividly recreated through the barely audible sound of his wings, is a Biblical allusion come alive. And then the three social classes are effectively balanced through the linking of each to their style of dwelling: castle — the noble; mansion — the wealthy; cottage — the poor and the lowly.

One of Parliament's humanitarian orators could move, even if he might not alter, the feelings of those who opposed him. Bright was not much more successful in addressing the intellects of his countrymen with his economic arguments against the war. The fifty millions sterling needed to underwrite the Crimean campaign would be much better spent raising both the standard of living and the level of education of Englishmen. Not only will the expenditure of that much money for war mean a loss to the English people, but also the state of trade will be disturbed and that of finance deranged.[16] In *Maud* (1855) Tennyson put Bright's economic stand against the war in an unsympathetic light. The Manchester cotton manufacturer in search of peace is set down as a self-serving Quaker tradesman:

> Last week came one to the country town,
> To preach our poor little army down,
> And play the game of the despot king,
> Tho' the state has done it and thrice as well;
> This broad-brimm'd hawker of holy things
> Whose ear is cramm'd with his cotton, and rings
> Even in dreams to the chink of his pence,
> This huckster put down war! can he tell
> Whether war be a cause or a consequence?[17]

This is not the occasion to examine at great length Tennyson's opinion of Bright but a word need be said in explanation of the newly made Poet Laureate's disapproval. The poet who had written "The Charge of the Light Brigade" in 1854, in which duty is exalted though it mean certain death, might well despise a fellow Englishman who, possessor of a mercantile background, continued to remind his countrymen of the financial costs of war. Whatever Tennyson's own opinion of the relative merits of glory or gain, it is the spasmodic young man of *Maud* who makes the reference to Bright. In the context of the young man's despair the disparagement of Bright is more than a gratuitous Tennysonian intrusion. Looking at mid-century England, the hero of *Maud* is distressed by the cash nexus relationship which has made every man the enemy of every other and led to commercial war as the modern state of nature:

> Why do they prate of the blessings of peace?
> we have made them a curse,
> Pickpockets, each hand lusting for all that
> is not its own;
> And lust for gain, in the spirit of Cain,
> is it better or worse
> Than the heart of the citizen hissing in war
> on his own hearthstone?
>
> But these are the days of advance, the works
> of the men of mind,
> When who but a fool would have faith in a
> tradesman's ware or his word?
> Is it peace or war? Civil war, as I think,
> and that of a kind
> The viler, as underhand, not openly bearing
> the sword [*ll*. 21–28].

Even a foreign war is better than that kind of peace. It would put a stop to that mammonish activity which has made Englishmen atoms in the aggregate instead of a society of men held together by a sense of national purpose. If an enemy man-of-war sailed up the Thames and fired a shot, all England would come together, in spirit; even the "smooth-faced, snub-nosed rogue would leap from his counter and till, / And strike if he could, were it but with his cheating yardwand, home" (lines 51–52). Tennyson's young man is not a misfit so much as a cast off from this social system: he has not rejected it; it has rejected him after the suicide of his father following a speculation which failed. His prospects ruined, the hero of *Maud* could not marry his childhood love. Unable to compete according to his society's dictates, he goes off to the Black Sea believing that war can still ennoble "hearts in a cause." Small wonder then that Tennyson's morbid young man rails at a Quaker cotton manufacturer who talks peace but who does not comprehend that the Crimean War is a "consequence" of the kind of peace that has been so profitable to the men in Bright's commercial circles. [18]

A recent historian has pointed out that Bright's opinion that the Crimean War was a mistake has landed in the history books. From that, it is not difficult to generalize that all wars are wrong. To quote from A.J.P. Taylor about Bright's influence is to justify the overall time span of this study. Our human memory may be short but we are after all not so very far away from mid-century Victorian England: "It is no accident that Bright at the end of his life, had Joseph Chamberlain as his colleague in the representation of Birmingham. There was a continuity of ideas from Bright to Joseph Chamberlain; and from Joseph Chamberlain to Neville. The Munich settlement of 1938 was implicit in Bright's opposition to the Crimean War. I am not sure whether this condemns Bright's attitude or justifies Munich."[19]

For another generation, Bright continued in his denunciation of war and the principle of the armed nation. In a letter to Pietro Sbarbaro, a reply to an invitation to attend the Peace Congress of 1878 in Savona, he struck out against the expense of standing armies: "The situation of Europe at this moment is deplorable; its nations are groaning under the weight of enormous armies and burdensome taxation. They are at the same time disjoined in interests and sentiments by tariffs, which form an insurmountable barrier between the peoples of the different States, and prevent that reciprocity of interests which would make it impossible for their statesman to drag them into war."[20] The gravest issues before the nations of Europe are the demobilization of standing armies and the avoidance of war. Bright's insistence upon free trade as a panacea looks ahead to the Common Market and still ahead to a United Europe: "If tariffs were abolished, or even if they were made very moderate, the nations would trade freely with each other, their

13

commerce would increase enormously, and they would bit by bit become like one grand nation; their commercial interests would multiply on such a scale and their natural knowledge and intercourse would become so intimate, that the ambition of monarchs and of statesmen would be impotent to drive them to war."[21] What hinders Europe from making such a move which would rid her of the menace of war and the ruinous cost of standing armies? It is the commercial interests who support the principle of large armies: "Monopoly in commerce, high tariffs, protection of the trading classes at the expense of society and the consumers, such are the allies of great armies and the grand obstacle to a general and lasting peace in Europe. Destroy the tariffs, or reduce them greatly, and standing armies will be dissolved, for then almost every pretext on which they are kept up will have disappeared."[22]

Two years earlier at the beginning of the agitation over the Eastern Question of 1876–1878, Bright singled out more pointedly the special interests who benefited materially by war. He urged working men not to be taken in by that influence, for ultimately it is they who suffer in a variety of ways from hostilities. Those whose living is made through money spent for armaments are anxious to keep up the war spirit. On November 25, 1876, Bright replied to a letter written by Bristol working men asking whether they should demonstrate in support of the Christian populations of Turkey in Bulgaria, some of whom had been barbarously put to death by the Turks. Despite the Bulgarian atrocities, demonstrations against Turkey were considered unpatriotic because a voice against Turkey was interpreted as a voice for Russia, who wanted to intervene on behalf of her oppressed fellow slavs, the Bulgarians. Bright wrote:

> You should condemn this foolish and wicked jealousy of Russia, which springs from ignorance among our people, and is fostered by writers in the press. It suits those who live out of the 25,000,000 £ spent annually, and for the most part wasted on our monstrous armaments, to keep up this feeling, and the influential

14

among them are constantly acting on the proprietors, editors, and writers of the London newspapers. Working men everywhere should resist this feeling and influence. It is their blood which is shed in war; the destruction of capital and the injury to industry and trade fall upon them with crushing weight. But for the wicked wars of past time, which now we all see to have been wicked, the working classes of this country might have been surrounded by the comforts of home and blessed with education, as are the families of what is termed the middle classes of our English society.[23]

The latter half of the nineteenth century was a time of "little wars." In 1882 England's involvement in Egyptian affairs had led to the bombardment of Alexandria. Once again in a letter, Bright explained his anti-war attitude, reflecting that only those who make money from wars will support them. Accused by the press of being in favor of "peace at any price" and being in opposition not just to the "Egyptian war in particular, but all wars," Bright replied to a correspondent:

> The *Spectator* and other supporters of this war answer me by saying that I oppose this war because I condemn all war. The same thing was said during the Crimean War.
> I have not opposed any war on the ground that all war is unlawful and immoral. I have discussed these questions of war, Chinese, Crimean, Afghan, Zulu, Egyptian on grounds common to and admitted by all thoughtful men, and have condemned them with arguments which I believe never have been answered.
> I will not discuss the abstract question. I shall be content when we reach the point at which all Christian men will condemn war when it is unnecessary, unjust and leading to no useful or good result. We are far from that point now, but we make some way towards it.
> ...
> Perhaps the bondholders and those who have made money by [war], and those who have got promotion, and titles and pensions, will defend it but thoughtful and Christian men will condemn it.[24]

Two years later and almost at the end of Bright's life, his arguments against war unheeded, Europe is arming. Writing to an American Quaker in 1884, the textile manufacturer and apostle of free trade desires that America will never know war again. In contrast, Europe is bristling with weapons; and since they have them, nations will be inclined to use them: "The question of peace ... claims the sympathy of all Christian nations. On your continent we may hope your growing millions may henceforth know nothing of war.... Europe, unhappily, is a great camp. All its nations are armed, as if each expected an invasion from its neighbors, unconscious, apparently, that great armies tempt to war the moment any cause of dispute arises. The potentates and governments of Europe, I doubt not, dread war. They seek to guard themselves against it by enormous armaments." [25]

When he died in 1889, Bright was buried near the Friends' Meeting House in Rochdale. A recent biographer sums up his career thus: "Home rulers, imperialists, feminists, xenophobes, jingoes, and protectionists had lost a fierce enemy. Democrats, humanitarians, advocates of the arbitration of international disputes, free traders, Indians, Americans, and the Irish people lost a strong friend." [26]

Two

Her Majesty's Clerk
of the Privy Council

In *The Crown of Wild Olive* (1866), John Ruskin recommended the work of a writer for whom he had the highest esteem: "I pray all of you who have not read, to read with the most earnest attention Mr. Helps' two essays, on War and Government in the first volume of the last series of *Friends in Council* [1859]. Everything that can be argued against war is there simply, exhaustively, and most graphically stated. And all, there urged is true."[1] To Ruskin, Arthur Helps was "that most thoughtful writer" belonging in the company of the greatest. Listing things to be studied in *The Elements of Drawing* (1857), Ruskin reminded himself, "Of reflective prose, read chiefly Bacon, Johnson, and Helps."[2] In the third volume of *Modern Painters* (1856), Helps is put with other eminent embodiments of "Man Thinking": "A true thinker who has practical purpose in his thinking and is sincere, as Plato, or Carlyle, or Helps, becomes in some sort a seer, and must be always of infinite use in his generation."[3] In a gesture of mutual esteem, Helps dedicated another book on war, his *Conversations on War and General Culture* (1871), to Ruskin.

After Cobden and Bright, Helps presents us with the awareness of a man of letters. Cobden wrote political pamphlets and Bright, political speeches and public letters. Helps wrote literary essays. Cobden and Bright were public men; Helps spent much of his life as a private secretary until made clerk of the privy council in 1860. Bright uses the dispatches from the Crimea to recreate the suffering of the wounded and the dying; the bookish Helps selects a descrip-

17

tion of the carnage of war from Book IV of *Gulliver's Travels*. In sum, Helps' writings on war are reflective. He is not the anti-war politician seeking to move the public to the virtuous action of ending a war not wholly unpopular.

Reminscent of the method of Dryden in his *Essay on Dramatic Poesy*, Helps' writings on war take the form of conversations between friends, except Helps' "friends" do not stand for different points of view so much as they represent several facets of one man's viewpoint divided among a set of agreeable speakers who do not challenge each other overmuch. Coming under discussion are questions about who promotes war and who benefits by it. The problem of standing armies is not ignored. On the one hand, the conversationalists are meliorists in their belief that civilization will evolve to a point where war will no longer be a part of human affairs. On the other hand, the speakers are realistic in observing that Europe is far from ready to disarm.

Despite the likely influence of his proximity and access to the politically powerful as clerk of the privy council, Helps assigned cultural not political reasons for the promotion of war. Wars are occasioned by "dullness" in the heads of state. "War is a most interesting game; and those who have the power of playing at it, will play at it unless they can be interested in some other way." One of the "friends in council" then substitutes "want of culture" for "dullness" and, with a suggestion of Matthew Arnold's "Barbarians," the ruling classes who have sweetness but little light, he reminds his listeners of the perpetual benightedness of those who control the destinies of nations:

> In any great war there are about twenty or thirty persons who may be charged with having been the prime movers of it. They are, for the most part, kings, statesmen, diplomatists, writers, great speakers. Most of them are middle-aged or elderly gentlemen. According to the average value of life, they have about twelve or fifteen years expectation of it. One would really think that they might employ these ... years a little better than in concerning themselves with war. But the real fact is, that most of

them, except the writers, are very ignorant. They know nothing of Science; they know nothing of Literature; of real statesmanship, too, very little. Many of them, I daresay, have scarcely realized the fact of which Science has informed us, that this planet is a very small and insignificant body, and that to rule over a little more or less of it is not a thing to be proud or ashamed of.[4]

And who benefits by war? To Helps, it is the heads of state who make war; those who stand to gain materially by it are listed as obligingly necessary appendages for implementing foreign policy: "War may be useful to contractors, armourers, the population of some seaport towns and arsenals, occassionally to certain classes of ship owners and merchants, and generally to those through whose hands the money raised for war passes."[5]

If we are to judge what a writer deems important not by what he tells us he thinks is important in the language of intellectual abstraction, but by the degree to which what lies closest to his pulse emerges in concrete language, then it is on the subject of standing armies that we catch an intimation of why Ruskin, one of the greatest prose masters, held Helps in such high esteem. Standing armies are a temptation to war. Here, Helps rises above the commonplace through the rhetorical force of his analogies:

As some excuse for monarchs, we must own that the natural disposition of mankind is to make use of whatever they possess, whether it be advisable to use it or not. The man who has the gift of eloquence cannot bear an enforced silence, however injurious to himself it may be for him to speak out.... The man who has the rare faculty of exquisite expression will write books, though the writing of books is, as some think, the most deplorable occupation, except grinding metals or working in a coal-pit, that has yet been invented by human beings.... Hence the man who has half a million of soldiers to play with is grievously tempted to use them, whether the use be wise or not. You might nearly as well trust a child with a large whip, and expect him not to slash about with in in a most inconsiderate manner as to expect a man who has at his command immense armies (perhaps an hereditary

19

acquisition) not to do something with them, however un-called-for that something may be.[6]

Not only is the rhetoric above the commonplace, but also the length to which Helps is willing to carry his argument is unusual for Victorian England, more inclined to be roused by the sentiments of the ode to military duty played upon in the Poet Laureate's "The Charge of the Light Brigade." To begin with, there should be a limit to the amount of military expenditure in support of *any* ruler: "...I venture to ask the simple question whether there is any dynasty on earth that is worth maintaining at the cost of keeping up an army of five hundred thousand soldiers."[7] And in response to the In-vasionists' panics, he carries his argument as far as it will go. If there is a continuity between Bright and Neville Chamberlain, there is also a continuity between Helps and the "Rather red than dead" position of our time. Rather England be invaded than put out enormous outlays for a standing army and a Fortress Britannia. Af-ter all, many a great nation has been invaded even sometimes to its advantage:

> In speaking of the subject of war, it is natural to think espe-cially of one's own country, and, in doing so, to consider that apprehension of invasion which periodically besets the English. It is surely right that they should sometimes entertain, and very gravely entertain, this apprehension. But it need not become a bugbear. Let me ask what great nation has not been invaded? Were not the Greeks invaded by the Persians, the Romans by the Carthaginians, the Swiss by the Burgundians: and with what result in each case history declares. There would be much calamity — there might (I firmly believe there would) result great honour from our being invaded; there certainly would be no shame in the mere fact of invasion; and the fear of such an event ought not lead to any needless outlay of money which ... had better "fructify in the pockets of the people."[8]

Such an antidote for the invasion jitters is at best equivocal. It might be said that Helps' speaker is not averse to invasion but says

20

nothing about conquest. The Romans were invaded by Hannibal but they ultimately leveled Carthage and sowed salt all over the ruins. Nowhere does Helps' speaker hit at the spirit of a British corporal of World War II: Let them invade, we shall prevail. But even to suggest that England could stand an invasion whether she should repel the invader or fall seems out of place in mid-Victorian England, lately beset by an invasion panic and heir to a fear of invasion by France dating at least as far back as the era of Defoe's *Review*. However extreme his argument, Helps intended it to support the following proposition: since it is patently impossible to make England unassailable, it behooves her government to be moderate both in providing for an army and in constructing defenses. Sir Robert Peel would in all probability have rejected Helps' argument but supported his proposition by his own statement that in times of peace England must "consent to incur some risk" rather than spend vast sums on military preparedness.

We can only wonder whether Queen Victoria was acquainted with the work of the clerk to the privy council appointed to that position in 1860, the year after his essay on war was in print. Judging by the editorial work she permitted Helps to do — revising Prince Albert's speeches for publication in 1862 and preparing for the press the accounts of Her Majesty's travels in Scotland — her confidence in him was assured; or perhaps she neither knew of nor could take seriously a defeatist attitude that was not to gain converts until our century.

It may be that Helps' "friends in council" could entertain the prospect of invasion because they would have liked to believe that it would never take place. On the optimistic side, they trust in the power of opinion and the force of evolution to do away with war. Unbounded is their faith in a monarch's willingness to abide by the wish of his subjects: "Why Haman could not bear the existence of one man, Mordecai, who sat at the king's gate, and did not do honour to Haman."[9] Surely to ignore public opinion, a monarch must be an exceptional personage, exceptional enough to conclude for himself that wars are detrimental to a nation's general well-being. Men of reason and good will must work to shape that opinion by writing against the evils of war confident that "...in good time some grand result will come of all our labours which hitherto appear to have been so lamentably fruitless.... Jean Paul says, 'The frogs cease croaking when a light is placed on the banks of the pond.' That is all you want — light — and a great many things besides the croaking of frogs ... will cease when once a sufficient light is brought to bear upon them."[10] To an enlightened national opinion, Helps would add an emerging international opinion. Echoing Tennyson's "the Parliament of man, the Federation of the world" in "Locksley Hall," he projected a League of Nations as keeper of the peace: "Again, there is a much greater power of combination than there ever was before, not only amongst people of the same race and country but throughout the whole civilized world. It is not impossible that great leagues and associations may yet be formed amongst the principal peoples of the world, having for their object to put a restraint upon the intolerable burdens and miseries of needless wars."[11]

Even so. But besides the protest of reasonable men as an influence upon national and world opinion, the forces of evolution are ever present. War will become obsolete as other evils have done in the past: "...we may take some comfort from what has happened in the world's history in similar cases. There has been some great evil — some world wide folly — such as duelling, or judicial torture, or persecution for religious opinions. The horrid evil has gone on, apparently without any abatement in many generations, when all of a sudden the evil thing has fallen away from mankind, like a garment which no longer fits, and you are unable to say, 'who has done this?' "[12]

Helps' conversationalists agree to the possibilities of the future but they do not end their discussion buoyed with the prospects of peace with the "Hail to the Future!" found at the end of Bertha von Suttner's hopeful *Lay Down Your Arms*. Whatever ought to be, a realistic appraisal of the situation of Europe leads to the inescapable conclusion that nations are not ready to disarm in 1871. "...[I]n the present state of Europe it is verging on the Utopian to imagine that you can persuade any two or three of the principal nations to agree to a reduction in armaments. I do not say the time may not come, when ... pacific theories may possibly enter into practice; but surely the present is not that time."[13] And lest that judgment seem topically influenced by the continental military adventures of 1871, Helps casts a backward glance over the centuries and ends with an even more somber judgment of human nature. No western nation has behaved in a Christian manner to another in the history of Christianity: "It is now 1871 years since Our Saviour came into this world. During that time there have been a great many individual Christians, or, at any rate, persons who believed that they conformed to the dictates of their Great Master. But you will find it hard to maintain that there has been one Christian nation, if we may judge its claims to Christianity by its conduct towards other nations."[14]

Three
Ars Vincit Omnia

In 1865 John Ruskin offered a lecture on war to the Royal Military Academy at Woolwich. At the beginning, the art critic reveals an extraordinary talent for arousing the interest of this audience when he proposes to elaborate upon the importance of war to art:

> ...I have given a considerable part of my life to the investigation of Venetian painting; and the result of that enquiry was my fixing upon one man as the greatest of all Venetians, and therefore, as I believed, of all painters whatsoever. I formed this faith ... in the supremacy of the painter Tintoret under a roof covered with his pictures; and of those pictures, three of the noblest were then in the form of shreds of ragged canvas, mixed up with the laths of the roof, rent through by three Austiran shells. Now it is not every lecturer who *could* tell you that he had seen three of his favourite pictures torn to rags by bomb-shells. And after such a sight, it is not every lecturer who *would* tell you that, nevertheless, war was the foundation of all great art.[1]

It is easy to visualize Ruskin in Italy looking at three shell torn paintings but not to comprehend at first why he should continue in the praise of war. Ruskin was not always consistent in his statements about war. What he has said in support of it has been forgotten; what he has said against it has remained in the consciousness of the nineteenth and twentieth centuries in two ways. First, his grasp of the commercial aspect of war led him to single out for blame a class, the capitalists. Second, his own motto, if any, being "there is no wealth but life," he raised and discussed at length the issue of national priorities.

It would not do to pass over Ruskin's attitude in support of war because that omission would serve only to perpetuate the notion that he, being anti-capitalist in economics, was a patron saint of the Socialist movement with its international leanings and therefore against anything but class war. He was aware that he had spoken both for and against war throughout his writings. As a particular example of his pro-war feeling, he thought that the Crimean War was "productive of good more than evil" and that if it were possible to ask those who suffered most they would reply with a sob and a war cry, "Set on."[2]

To the cadets at the Royal Military Academy Ruskin displayed a pro-war side when he set a case for the dependence of art upon war: "...all the pure and noble arts are founded on war; no great art ever yet rose on earth, but among a nation of soliders. There is no art among shepherd people, if it remains at peace. There is no art among an agricultural people, if it remains at peace. Commerce is barely consistent with fine art; but cannot produce it. Manufacture not only is unable to produce it, but invariably destroys whatever seeds of it exist. There is no great art possible to a nation but that which is based on battle."[3] It is beside the point to dispute here Ruskin's argument that martial nations produce great art; but it is important to pursue a reconciliation of his praise and blame of war. The military men Ruskin admired from personal acquaintance possessed a quiet courage and a sense of duty that he considered noble. Any institution that might produce such examples of humanity was a valuable asset to any society. Ruskin further reconciled war and peace by making war a class pursuit. He told his audience of officer trainees that war was the profession of the leisured classes of all nations. As long as battles were fought by them and only by them, war is noble and acceptable: "If you, the gentlemen of this or any other kingdom, choose to make your pastime of contest, do so, and welcome; but set not up these unhappy peasant-pieces upon the chequer of forest and field. If the wager is to be death, lay it on your own heads, not theirs."[4]

Part of Ruskin's opposition to war is rooted in its post-

Napoleonic, post-Clausewitzian character. In modern war men fight not in small professional armies as a warrior class for exercise and play and love of conquest but unwillingly, having been forced away from far more useful pursuits. Ruskin tells his audience of future leaders that a conscript army has no business in the field:

> If you take away masses of men from all industrial employment, – to feed them by the labour of others, – to provide them with destructive machines, varied daily in national rivalship of inventive cast; if you have to ravage the country which you attack, – to destroy, for a score of future years, its roads, its woods, its cities and its harbours: – and if finally having brought masses of men, counted by hundreds of thousands, face to face, you tear those masses to pieces with jagged shot, and leave the living countlessly beyond all help of surgery, to starve and parch, through days of torture, down to clots of clay – what book accounts shall record the cost of your work; – what book of judgments sentence the guilt of it.[5]

By analogy when the members of the ruling classes have a dispute, they do not send their footmen over to Battersea fields to fight each other. The matter is settled by laws of honor, not physical force; the private fight does not become a public brawl. That peasants should shoot each other over their masters' quarrel when – as in Hardy's turn of the century poem, "The Man He Killed" – they might have stood each other a drink under other circumstances is a crime. Such a condition of things reveals the "ghastly ludicrousness" of modern war. To illustrate the point that governing classes should confine war to themselves, Ruskin summons "the greatest of our English thinkers," Carlyle, whose Dumdrudge pronouncement was to become part of the working class consciousness:

> What, speaking in quite unofficial language, is the net purport and upshot of war? To my own knowledge, for example, there dwell and toil, in the British village of Dumdrudge, usually some five hundred souls. From these, by certain "natural enemies" of the French there are successively selected, during the French war, say

thirty able-bodied men: Dumdrudge, at her own expense, has suckled and nursed them: she has, not without difficulty and sorrow, fed them up to manhood, and even trained them to crafts, so that one can weave, another build, another hammer, and the weakest can stand under thirty stone avoirdupois. Nevertheless, amid much weeping and swearing, they are selected; all dressed in red; and shipped away, at the public charges, some two thousand miles or say only to the south of Spain; and fed there till wanted.

And now to that same spot in the south of Spain are thirty similar French artisans from a French Dumdrudge, in like manner wending; till at length, after infinite effort, the two parties come into actual juxtaposition; and Thirty stands fronting Thirty, each with a gun in his hand.

Straightaway the word "Fire!" is given, and they blow the souls out of one another; and in place of sixty brisk useful craftsmen, the world has sixty dead carcases, which it must bury, and anon shed tears. Had these men any quarrel? Busy as the Devil is, not the smallest! They lived far enough apart; were the entirest strangers; nay, in so wide a Universe, there was even, unconsciously, by Commerce, some mutual helpfulness between them. How then? Simpleton! their Governors had fallen out; and instead of shooting one another, had the cunning to make these poor blockheads shoot.[6]

That is not the way that the deadly game of the leisure classes ought to be played. War is their province alone; it ennobles them. Nor, Ruskin adds, are field sports a substitute. Better a tournament than a steeplechase. Better a knight earn his bread by sword play than by bat play at cricket. And better ride a war horse than bet on a race horse.[7]

One surmises that Ruskin's warrior class at play would fight only in a cause made just by the sanction of its code of honor. It is the war fought by the unwilling artisan to further the commerical ambitions of the capitalist class which is unjust and which brings forth in Ruskin the anit-war sentiment for which he is remembered in working class circles. Through his denunciations of the capitalist class, Ruskin contributed to the climate of opinion which led the

employed today on productive labour."[15] Political economy is silent in response to the proposal to use borrowed capitalist cash to build, for example, libraries, art galleries, and museums as an alternative to the "panic" France and England "buy of each other" by way of arms procurement.[16] What happens then is inevitable:

> The practical result of the absence of any such statement is, that capitalists, when they do not know what to do with their money, persuade the peasants, in various countries, that the said peasants want guns to shoot each other with. The peasants accordingly borrow guns, out of the manufacture of which the capitalists get percentage, and the men of science much amusement and credit. Then the peasants shoot a certain number of each other, until they get tired; and burn each other's houses down in various places. Then they put the guns back into towers, arsenals, etc., in ornamental patterns; (and the victorious party put also some ragged flags in churches). And then the capitalists tax both, annually, ever afterwards, to pay interest on the loan of the guns and gunpowder. And that is what capitalists call "knowing what to do with their money"; and what commercial men in general call "practical" as opposed to sentimental "Political Economy."[17]

Behind the capitalist, then, stands his false conscience, the political economist, whose economic laws sanction human greed and thus make war economically legitimate. Referring to the preparations for defense during the last of the three invasionist panics in 1860, Ruskin writes: "...at present, France and England purchase of each other ten millions sterling worth of consternation annually, a remarkably light crop, half thorns and half aspen leaves, — sown, reaped, and granaried by the 'science' of the modern political economist, teaching covetousness instead of truth."[18] In a more playfully ironical vein, Ruskin proposes that the eternal laws of the science of political economy be tested by putting the "war business" on a contract basis, employing the principle of accountability and payment by results:

> If our present doctrines of political economy be just, let us trust

31

them to the utmost; take the war business out of the government's hands and test therein the principles of supply and demand. Let our future sieges of Sebastopol be done by contract — no capture, no pay — (I admit that things might go better so); and let us sell the commands of our prospective battles, with our vicarages, to the lowest bidder; so may we have cheap victories and divinity. On the other hand, if we have so much suspicion of our science, that we dare not trust it on military or spiritual business, would it not be reasonable to try whether some authoritative handling may prosper in matters utilitarian?[19]

That last rhetorical question, can the government be persuaded to do things really useful, brings us to Ruskin's concern for reordering national priorities, a concern he never tired of reiterating. On one occasion, the author of *Modern Painters* could not resist dramatizing the absurd disproportion in the expenditures for art and war. In the *Pall Mall Gazette* of February 18, 1867, Ruskin read about a parliamentary debate over the expenditure of £164,000 for the Blacas collection of classical and early Christian antiquities. The next day's *Gazette* recorded the Army and Navy expenditure for 1866 at £24,000,000. One MP saw the money for the collection of antiquities to be a "danger to the national pockets." Omitting extra zeros for the sake of simplicity, Ruskin asks his readers to compare the two figures and proceeds to calculate the disparity between them: "But calculate the proportion of these two sums, and then imagine to yourself the beautiful state of rationality of any private gentleman, who, having regretfully spent £164 on pictures for his walls, paid willingly £24,000 annually to the policeman who looked after his shutters! You practical English! — will you ever unbar the shutters of your brains, and hang a picture or two in *those* state-chambers?"[20]

The expenses of governments are all high; even so, it costs less to build a ship to carry timber instead of cannon, or coal for kitchen fires instead of, to employ the military jargon of the day, "liquid hostile fire." But if nations want to go to war, they will find their governments ready to oblige and put on the hat of one of those whom Aristophanes called "shield-sellers": "And when ... the shields take the form of iron ships, with apparatus 'for defense against liquid fire,' as I see by latest accounts they are now arranging the decks in English dockyards — they become costly biers enough for the grey convoy of chief-mourner waves, wreathed with funereal foam, to bear back the dead upon; the massy shoulders of those corpse bearers being intended for quite other work, and to bear the living, and food for the living, if we would let them."[21]

What are a nation's priorities? Do a people want materials for life or munitions for death? In the "Store-keeping" chapter of *Munera Pulveris*, Ruskin asks about the nature of a nation's store. Have the right or wrong things been worked for and gathered? The quality of the nation's existence depends upon the answer, as Ruskin shows in the following example of guns displacing butter in a hypothetical nation's economy:

> For example, let us imagine a society, of no great extent, occupied in procuring and laying up store of corn, wine, wool, silk, and other such preservable materials of food and clothing; and that it has a currency representing them. Imagine farther, that on days of festivity, the society, discovering itself to derive satisfaction from pyrotechnics, gradually turns its attention more and more to the manufacture of gunpowder; so that an increasing number of labourers, giving what time they can spare to this branch of industry, bring increasing quantities of combustibles into the store, and use the general orders received in exchange to obtain such wine, wool, or corn, as they may have need of. The currency remains the same, and represents precisely the same amount of material in the store, and of labour spent in producing it. But the corn and wine gradually vanish, and in their place, as gradually, appear sulphur and saltpetre, till at last the labourers who have consumed corn and supplied nitre, presenting on a festal morning some of their currency to obtain materials for the feast, discover that no amount of currency will command anything Festive, except Fire. The supply of rockets is unlimited, but that of food limited, in a quite final manner; and the whole currency in the hands of the society represents an infinite power of detonation but none of existence.[22]

Ruskin admits that the example above is an exaggeration and a *reductio ad absurdum* and that in actuality a rise in the price of food would check the process. Just the same his example "...falls short of the actual facts of human life in expression of the depth and intensity of the folly itself. For a greater part (the reader would not believe how great until he saw the statistics in detail) of the most earnest and ingenious industry of the world is spent in producing munitions of war; gathering, that is to say, the materials, not of festive, but of consuming fire; filling its stores with all power of the instruments of pain, and all affluence of the ministries of death."[23]

National priorities ought to be such that a government will borrow surplus capitalist cash and spend it encouraging the arts of peace. The transition will not be easy though. The social critic who wrote about servile and free workmen knew something about the nature of work. It is not a simple task to convert men from making things of no intrinsic worth, such as weapons, to creating something of value. The making of guns and bombs has, Ruskin fears, a sinister attraction all of its own irrespective of profit:

> We cannot be certain that all the labour spent on vanity has been diverted from reality, and that for every bad thing produced a precious thing has been lost. In great measure, the vain things represent the results of roused indolence; they have been carved, as toys, in extra time: and, if they had not been made, nothing else would have been made. Even to munitions of war this principle applies; they partly represent the work of men who, if they had not made spears, would never have made pruning-hooks, and who are incapable of any activities but those of contest.[24]

Four

The Treasurer of the Eastern Question Association

For all the attention he gave to the connection between capital and war Ruskin points to no specific instances. Not too many years were to lapse before his dictum — that capitalists support unjust wars — was to pass from the abstraction of intellectual statement to a political crisis made to prove his point. The occasion was the Eastern Question of 1876–1878, and the writer who was to advertise the degree of capitalistic involvement was William Morris.

In 1875, a year before Victoria was proclaimed "Empress of India," the Christian peoples of the Ottoman Empire rose in revolt against Turkish overlordship. The Bulgarians suffered the brunt of Turkish suppression in June 1876, English newspapers carried accounts of atrocities perpetrated by Turkish mercenaries. Since the victims were Slavs and Pan-Slavism was also in the air, Russia threatened to intervene on behalf of her oppressed cousins. The British government had bought 176,000 shares in the Suez Canal in 1875. Should Russia liberate the Christian provinces, she would constitute a greater presence in the Middle East, the gateway to India, than suited the British.

Since the Crimean War, England had propped the crumbling Ottoman Empire; and despite officially substantiated revelations of atrocities, Disraeli's alliance with the Turks stood. Imperialist aims took precedence over moral imperatives. The Eastern Question Association was formed to promote resistance to Disraeli's Turkish policy. Among its well wishers were such literary figures as

35

Trollope, Browning, Carlyle, and Rossetti. William Morris was made the Treasurer of the Association in December, 1876.[1] Outraged by the behavior of his country's ministers, Morris had decided that to be an influence upon public affairs he had to do whatever was necessary to draw attention to his cause. Years later in another cause, he would take to the streets and get arrested for allegedly assaulting a policeman, but for now he would signal his entry into public life with a letter titled, "England and the Turks," written to the editor of the *Daily News* two months before he became an officer in the Association.

Morris begins his letter by noting that there is a rumor that England is going to war. Playing the ingenu, he states that a few weeks before, having heard the news of Turkish atrocities, he assumed that if the English were going to fight, it obviously would be against Turkish savagery, a course of action that would make every true-born Englishman proud of his native land. But no, awakening from his idealist's dream, he has discovered that England wants to go to war on the side of Turkey should Russia intervene on behalf of the murdered people of Bulgaria. At that point Morris puts by his feigned naïveté and rails at England's moral confusion: "Can history show a greater absurdity than this or greater fools than the English people will be if they do not make it clear to the Ministry and the Porte [Turkish government] that they will wage no war on behalf of the Turks, no war on behalf of thieves and murderers?"[2]

The party of imperialism, led by Disraeli and Victoria, bolstered the Turks because it envisioned greater British influence in the Middle East. In support of the Queen and her Prime Minister were elements who were out for more tangible gain, financial speculators who fueled the newspapers with anti-Russian propaganda because they had invested £165,000,000 in depreciated Turkish bonds which had recently been put on the market. Carlyle may have had that transaction in mind when he summed up his opinion of the Eastern Question in a letter to George Howard printed in the *Times* on November 28, 1876: "The only clear advice I have to give is ... that the unspeakable Turk should be immediately struck out of the question, and the country [Bulgaria] left to honest European guidance; delaying which can be profitable or agreeable only to gamblers on the Stock Exchange but distressing and unprofitable to all other men."[3]

Also aware of the the activities of speculators, the Council of the Labour Representation League printed on May 2, 1877, an address to the working classes advising them not to go to war to safeguard those investments: "English millionaires, who preferred to invest capital resulting from your labours in Turkish Bonds, rather than employ it in home speculation, should be taught your Lives and your Taxes should not be used for recovering their personal debts."[4]

Morris may have seen that passage not too long before he published his manifesto, "UNJUST WAR: To the Working-men of England," on May 11, 1877. If the English side with the Turks against Russia, Morris argued, it will not be to pay her back for misdeeds of the past, but to abet in the suppression of Turkey's Christian population. Such a move would be welcomed by English special interests: the idle class of jingoes who insist upon the abstraction of a "spirited foreign policy"; the guardians of India who want to forestall an invasion that might not occur in a century, if ever; the military men who are keen on displaying the might of the British Army and Navy to the peoples of Europe; and the holders of Turkish bonds who hope for a good return on their investment. Morris recapitualtes these categories of interests, gathering rhetorical force, identifying them more pointedly in language charged with the righteous fervor of a lover of justice: "And who are they who flaunt in our faces the banner inscribed on one side *English Interests*, and one the other *Russian Misdeeds*? Who are they that are leading us into war? Let us look at these saviours of England's honour, ... these scourges of Russia's iniquities! Do you know them? — Greedy gamblers on the Stock Exchange, idle officers of the army and navy (poor fellows!), worn out mockers of the Clubs, desperate purveyors of exciting war-news for the comfortable breakfast tables of those who have nothing to lose by war...."[5]

Morris's greatest scorn is reserved for the Tories, especially their leader, "that ancient place-hunter," Disraeli who, possessed of an "empty heart and shifty head," is leading England into confusion if not destruction. It is not the working man's fight: "O shame and double shame if we march under such a leadership as this in an unjust war against a people who are *not* our enemies, against Europe, against freedom, against nature, against the hope of the world."[6]

The tone of the manifesto reaches its highest pitch when Morris insinuates a note of class emnity. Those most desirous of pushing England into war are the rich who despise the working man and would gladly aid the capitalist in suppressing him: " — these men cannot speak of your order, of its aims, of its leaders without a sneer or an insult: these men, if they had the power (may England perish rather) would thwart your just aspirations, would silence you, would deliver you bound hand and foot for ever to irresponsible capital — and these men, I say it deliberately, are the heart and soul of the party that is driving us to an unjust war." He urges the working classes to rise from their lethargy and seek out the middle classes as allies, "...that we may all protest solemnly and perseveringly against our being dragged ... into an UNJUST WAR, in which, if we are victorious, we shall win shame, loss, and rebuke; and if we are overpowered — what then?[7]

It may be said that the agitation over the Eastern Question left two lasting imprints on English political history. For one, the war party made a statement of Disraeli's about the righteous war into a popular song, the jingoes' war cry, thereby adding a word to our political vocabulary:

> We don't want to fight, but by jingo if we do,
> We've got the ships, we've got the men, we've got the money, too.[8]

For another, the controversy transformed Morris, who described himself in his letter to the *Daily News* as a man who had heretofore gone about his life quietly, into an activist who spent a good part of the remainder of his life in the forefront of the Socialist cause.

Five

Dr. Strangelove, circa 1899

On August 29, 1898, much to the astonishment of Europe, Czar Nicholas II of Russia issued an invitation to all nations to confer over the limitations of armaments. "The Czar with an olive branch ... that's something new in history," commented a Viennese newspaper.[1] The pronouncement from Russia obsserved that despite the yearning for peace over the past twenty years particularly, "the intellectual and physical strength of nations, labour and capital alike, have been unproductively consumed in building terrible engines of destruction."[2]

Writing to Eduard Bertz on September 4, 1898, George Gissing outlined a new novel he was writing and also indicated his surprise at the Czar's move: "In the book I am going to write, the question of Peace will be involved. It is a love story, but with large issues — philosophic ... and cosmopolitan. The name is to be: 'The Crown of Life.' ... I don't know what to think of the Czar. It is so difficult to credit an aristocrat with high humanity. But the declaration undoubtedly has great importance." One English reaction to the Czar's call for peace was the formation of the Peace Crusade. On January 17, 1899, Gissing wrote another letter to Bertz announcing the completion of his new book which, in addition to its love story "...contains a rather vigourous attack on militarism. I have had to say hard things of all countries." Having anticipated the Czar's proposal, Gissing believed himself to be something of a prophet but was sensitive to possible criticism about having made the book to order so to take advantage of the peace movement: "A strange thing that the writing of a book should be finished just when the 'Peace Crusade' is becoming active. I planned the story more than a year ago. Still more oddly, Russia has a great part in it. But it is not the first time that my thoughts have anticipated public tendencies. Of course everyone will think I have sat down in a hurry to write an opportune book." Two weeks earlier, he had written to H. G. Wells calling *The Crown of Life* "an Antijingo book."[3]

Gissing's novel takes up the questions of peace, jingoism, and the role of the press as a fomenter of war. But Gissing was a novelist as well as a social critic, and it is in the creation of the character of Lee Hannaford that he fixes attention upon an aspect of industrial civilization at the end of the nineteenth century. Hannaford is one of those men who, as Ruskin put it, "if they had not made spears, would never have made pruning-hooks." He is the armaments technologist with a zest for destruction.

It is a tribute to the human imagination that the belief in the inevitability of peace could exist in an era that from 1884 to the end of the century saw the perfection of the repeating rifle, smokeless powder, the machine gun, and the quick-firing artillery piece.[4] Some sense of that progress and regression is present in *The Crown of Life* in a conversation between Piers Otway, an English merchant of Odessa, and Irene Derwent:

> We ought to be rapidly outgrowing warfare; isn't that the obvious next step in civilization? It seems a commonplace that everyone should look to that end, and strive for it. Yet we are going back — there's a militiary reaction — fighting is glorified by everyone who has a loud voice, and in no country more than in England. I wish you could hear a Russian friend of mine speak about it, a rich man who has just given up everything to join the Dukhobortsi. I never knew before what religious passion meant. And it seems to me that this is the world's only hope — peace made a religion. The forms don't matter; only let the supreme end be peace. It is what people have talked so much about — the religion of the future.[5]

By allowing Piers Otway to address himself to both sides of

the question, to both the possibility of peace and the likelihood of war, Gissing does not do justice to the full force of optimism behind the "question of Peace" he proposed to undertake in the novel, as that optimisim existed in the 1890's. For that feeling we need to turn to Berta von Suttner's semi-autobiographical anti-war novel, *Die Waffen nieder* (*Lay Down Your Arms*), which appeared in 1889. Born in 1843, the Harriet Beecher Stowe of the Peace Movement, as Tolstoy considered her, was the daughter of an Austrian lieutenant field-marshal. She nearly served as Alfred Nobel's secretary in 1876 but marriage to von Suttner changed her plans. She saw Nobel again in 1887 and in 1892 persuaded him to attend the Berne Peace Conference. After publication of her novel, she was active in the Peace Movement and was awarded the Nobel Peace Prize in 1905.[6]

The anti-war feeling in *Lay Down Your Arms* is directed at the statesmen and the generals who are imbued with the spirit of war and the will to fight. The central figure of the novel, Martha von Tilling, is the daughter of a retired Austrian general. Throughout the book runs a debate between father and daughter on the subject of war, the daughter regularly contradicting her father's militarism even to the extraordinary length of urging him to curse war as he lies dying of the cholera brought by invading Prussians.

Martha loses her first husband in the Austro-Italian war of 1859. Her second husband, also a career soldier, serves in the Schleswig-Holstein war, the Austro-Prussian war of 1866, and is wrongfully executed as a spy by the Communards after the Franco-Prussian war. Shouldering her personal losses, Martha then devotes her life to the cause of disarmament and international peace.

It is after her first husband is killed in action that the consciousness of the field-marshal's daughter undergoes a change. The scales fall off her eyes, and she becomes convinced that peace is not merely the absence of war, as cold is the absence of heat, but a positive state toward which the forces of history and evolution are driving. A reading of Buckle's *History of Civilization in England* assures her that the march not of the soldier but of the intellect has profoundly affected the evolution of man. As the world progresses, love of war will cool:

> One thing, however, was clear to me even then: that the history of mankind was not decided by, as the old theory taught, kings and statesmen, nor by the wars and treaties that were created by the greed of the former or the cunning of the latter, but by the gradual development of the intellect. The chronicle of courts and battles which are strung together in the history book represent isolated phenomena of the condition of culture at those epochs, not the cause of those conditions. Of the old-fashioned admiration with which other historical writers are accustomed to relate the lives of mighty conquerers and devastators of countries, I could find absolutely nothing in Buckle. On the contrary, he brings proof that the estimation in which the warrior class is held is in inverse ratio to the height of culture which the nation has reached; the lower you go in the barbaric past, the more frequent are the wars of the time, the narrower the limits of peace, province against province, city against city, family against family. He lays stress on the fact that, as society progresses, not only war itself, but the love of war will be found to diminish. That word spoke to my innermost heart.[7]

Fortified by that revelation, Martha works for peace together with her second husband who is persuaded that the little wars of the continent to which he, as a career officer, has had to muster, bloody as they are with the advent of improved weaponry, are merely little eddies in the mainstream of human evolution. Thus the book can end with a Hail to the Future! and a belief in the settlement of international disputes by a court of arbitration.[8]

Gissing's "peace made a religion" would be a welcome evolutionary development. But less hopeful indicators are overwhelming. One of those is the spirit of jingoism and another the arrogance of the press through which the "roaring of the Jingoes" can be heard. Gissing sees the English national character degenerating owing to imperialist attitudes and money worship. Like Shaw at the beginning of the First World War, he sees no difference between Prussian Junkerdom and English Junkerdom.

Dr. Strangelove, circa 1899

Comparing England and Germany, one of Gissing's characters expresses his "...fear that our brute, blustering Bismarck may be coming" (*Crown*, p. 180).

Pier Otway's brother Alexander is caricatured as a newspaperman who is a fervent advocate of "England über Alles," the land to which the whole creation moves. Englishmen are the "top of creation"; other races are "A poor lot! A shabby lot!" Lecturing Piers on the power of English journalism, Alexander boasts, "we English newspapermen have the destiny of the world in our hands. It makes me proud when I think of it. We guard the national honour. Let any confounded foreigner insult England, and he has to reckon with *us*. A word from *us*, and it means war, Piers, glorious war, with triumphs for the race and for civilization! England means civilization; the other nations don't count" (*Crown*, p. 51). When Piers, whose cosmopolitanism is an outgrowth of his enterprise in Odessa, objects, his bother accuses him of being a Little Englander who wants to keep England tame, when she must be prepared to fight: "No, no; we must be armed and triple-armed; we must be so strong that not all the confounded foreigners leagued together can touch us. It's the cause of civilization, Piers. I preach it whenever I get the chance.... I stand for England's honour. England's supremacy on sea and land" (*Crown*, pp. 51–52).[9]

When the next major war breaks out, profit seeking newspapers will be to blame, explains Piers to Irene: "There are newspaper proprietors in every country, who would slaughter half mankind for the pennies of the half who were left, without caring a fraction of a penny whether they had preached war for a truth or lie" (*Crown*, p. 158). Irene naively states that the press only mirrors public opinion, to which Piers replies, "I'm afraid it manufactures opinion, and stirs up feeling. Consider how very few people know or care anything about most subjects of international quarrel. The business of newspapers, in general, is to give a show of importance to what has no real importance at all — to prevent the world from living quietly — to arouse bitterness when the natural man would be quite indifferent" (*Crown*, p. 158).

43

At one point, the subject of war and the press leaves the discussion stage and stirs Gissing's creative impulse. It would almost appear that Gissing takes himself to task for neglecting his craft. Burning as any issue might be, it is the business of the novelist to dramatize social criticism and not use it as the stuff of long conversations verging on the essay.

Piers Otway's father, a mid-nineteenth century radical who named his son after Langland's plowman, left among his papers a satire on both the press and weapons research as instigators of war. It is a tale of two Asiatic kingdoms whose long peace was disturbed by the ambitions of their statesmen:

> We are told that a General in the army of Duroba, having a turn for experimental chemistry, had discovered a substance of terrible explosive power, which, by the exercise of further ingenuity, he had adapted for use in warfare. About the same time, a public official in Kalaya, whose duty it was to convey news to the community by means of a primitive system of manuscript placarding, hit upon a mechanical method whereby news sheets could be multiplied very rapidly and be sold to readers all over the kingdom. Now the Duroban General felt eager to test his discovery in a campaign, and, happening to have a quarrel with a politician in the neighbouring state, did his utmost to excite hostile feeling against Kalaya. On the other hand, the Kalayan official, his cupidity excited by the profits already arising from his invention, desired nothing better than some stirring event which would lead to still greater demand for the news sheets he distributed, and so he also was led to the idea of stirring up international strife. To be brief, these intrigues succeeded only too well; war was actually declared, the armies were mustered and marched to the encounter [*Crown*, p. 177].

The armies on either side debate the prospect of war by their campfires. The Durobans decide that they do not want to be killed" ... to please our General with the turn for chemistry" (*Crown*, p. 178). The Kalayans decide that if the statesmen on both sides are as angry as the news sheets relate, then they should fight each

44

Dr. Strangelove, circa 1899

other. Thus ended the war. Those responsible for its outbreak were given a punishment reminiscent of that meted out to criminals in Anthony Burgess' *Clockwork Orange*: exposure to a surfeit of the simulation of their crimes:

> The Duroban General, having been duly tried for a crime against his country, was imprisoned in a spacious building, the rooms of which were hung with great pictures representing every horror of battle with the ghastliest fidelity; here he was supplied with the materials for chemical experiment, to occupy his leisure, and very shortly, by accident, blew himself to pieces. The Kalayan publicist was also convicted of treason against the state; they banished him to a desert island, where for many hours daily he had to multiply copies of his news sheet — that issue which contained the declaration of war — and at evening burn them all. He presently became imbecile, and so passed away [*Crown*, p. 178].

The attenuated discussion and the apologue are flaws in the fabric of Gissing's novel. It would take a Dostoevsky to make a virtue of those elements in fiction. Gissing is at his best when he remains in the province of the novelist by creating a character as the vehicle for an idea. Had Gissing had sufficient inspiration to have made Lee Hannaford a major figure, he would have anticipated in *The Crown of Life* not only the Czar's proclamation but also "Dr. Strangelove." Hannaford is a weapons collector of the paramilitary mentality and a student of the chemistry of explosives. We first hear about him indirectly through a conversation between Arnold Jacks, his father John Jacks, and Piers Otway. Arnold Jacks' moral shallowness is brought to light by his exultation over the talents of Hannaford, among whose fascinations is a plan to turn Ireland into a military and naval base to be used entirely for that function. Hannaford's home is a "museum of modern weapons — a regular armoury." He has invented a new gun and a new explosive.

Arnold Jacks believes Hannaford to be a proper son of John Bull: "He showed me, by sketch and diagrams how many men he could kill within a given space.... What would become of us if we left all that kind of thing to the other countries? Hannaford is a patriot. He struck me as quite disinterested; personal gain is nothing to him. He loves his country, and is using his genius in her service" (*Crown*, p. 12). John Jacks contradicts his son who is taken by the novelty of the armaments technologist. The elder Jacks will not tolerate the idea of Hannaford as the new man on the English cultural scene: "...we talk very much, and very badly; in pulpit, and Parliament and press. We want the man who has something new to say, and knows how to say it. For my part, I don't think, when he comes, that he will glorify explosives. I want someone to talk about Peace — and *not* from the commercial point of view. The slaughterers shan't have it all their own way ... civilization will be too strong for them, and if old England doesn't lead in that direction, it will be her shame to the end of history" (*Crown*, p. 13).

A description of Hannaford's inner sanctum offers a glimpse of him as a collector of battlefield relics and accounts for the epithet "grave comedian," given Gissing by Mabel Donnelly. A survey of the artifacts in his room, besides providing an index to his mind, indicates that he is intended not so much as a sinister figure but as a grotesque, a ludicrous demon:

> Mr. Hannaford's sanctum ... had character; it was hung about with lethal weapons of many kinds and many epochs, including a memento of every important war waged in Europe since the date of Waterloo. A smoke-grimed rifle from some battlefield was in Hannaford's view a thing greatly precious; still more, a bayonet with stain of blood; these relics appealed to his emotions. Under glass were ranged minutiae such as bullets, fragments of shells, bits of gore-drenched cloth or linen, a splinter of human bone — all ticketed with neat inscription. A bookcase contained volumes of military, works on firearms, treatises on (chiefly explosive) chemistry; several great portfolios were packed with maps and diagrams of warfare. Upstairs, a long garret served as laboratory, and here were ranged less valuable possessions; weapons to which some doubt attached, unbloody scraps of

accoutrements, also a few models of cannon and the like [*Crown*, pp. 15–16].

For a time Hannaford endures the adversity that surrounds every struggling inventor. The English government is slow in coming to terms over an explosive device. Dr. Derwent, who has doubts about the inventor's sanity, remarks sardonically that it is a shame "...that an honest man who facilitates murder on so great a scale should be kept waiting for his reward!" (*Crown*, p. 84). Finally he makes his way in the world with a firm of manufacturers of explosives. His expertise is displayed in the newspapers on one occasion when he appraises a fellow inventor's new bullet: "Hannaford, writing with authority, criticised the invention; he gave particulars (the result of an experiment on an old horse) as to its mode of penetrating flesh and shattering bone; there was a gusto in his style, that of the true artist in bloodshed" (*Crown*, p. 202). Such a man who perfects a new gun or a new bullet is held in greater esteem than he who discovers a cure for diphtheria.

Hannaford's relationship with his wife reveals something of his Podsnappery and his near mad Strangelovian inclinations:

> Mrs. Hannaford was something of an artist; her husband spoke of all art with contempt—except the great art of human slaughter. She liked the society of foreigners; he, though a remarkable linguist, at heart, distrusted and despised all but English speaking folk. As a girl in her teens, she had been charmed by the man's virile accomplishments, his soldierly bearing and gay talk of martial things, though Hannaford was only a teacher of science. Nowadays she thought with dreary wonder of that fascination, and had come to loathe every trapping and habiliment of war. She knew him to be profoundly selfish, and recognized the other faults which hindered so clever a man from success in life; indolent habits, moral untrustworthiness, and a conceit which at times menaced insanity [*Crown*, p. 16].

In Hannaford, too, a curious sexlessness, perhaps impotence, accompanies his dreams of destruction, a pathological combination popularly ascribed to Adolph Hitler although Hitler was said to be lavishly courtly in his attentions to women in public: "Indeed he was not fond of the society of women, and grew less so every year. His tone with regard to them was marked with an almost puritanical coldness; he visited any feminine breach of the proprieties with angry censure.... His morality, in fact, no one doubted; the suspicions Mrs. Hannaford had once entertained when his coldness to her began, she now knew to be baseless. Absorbed in meditations on bloodshed and havoc, he held high the idea of chastity and in company agreeable to him, could allude to it as the safeguard of civil life" (*Crown*, p. 31).

The interesting dramatic potential of Hannaford is never fully realized. His occupation aside, we would like to know more about this Satanic man while we are treated to more than we need to know about the tepidly genteel major figures in the novel. Hannaford's part is peripheral to the plot which moves toward the eventual happiness of Piers Otway and Irene Derwent. When Hannaford appears it is generally to make himself disagreeable to his wife who is the aunt of Miss Derwent. As Gissing presents him, he is a caricature who moves in and out of the story eliciting hisses of "cad" and "villain." Beyond the plot, however, Hannaford has a symbolic function. He represents the spirit of those last fifteen years of the nineteenth century which witnessed the development in quick succession of rapid firing weaponry utilizing more powerful and efficient "propellants."[10] Regarded in that way, the figure of the armaments technologist becomes sinister. Though not clandestinely active promoting wars as his employers were later said to be, he and his co-workers in various countries, by virtue of human ingenuity, escalated technological progress in armaments, the progress of which the twentieth century has not seen the end.

Six

"The True Faith of the Armourer"

Over the half-century from the Crimean War to the Boer War, the Victorian writers we have examined have attributed the promotion of war to a variety of human agents: monarchs, statesmen, stock-jobbers, capitalists, and jingo journalists. At most the armourer was considered a willing accomplice of a government with a belligerent foreign policy. Although munitions makers had been operating on an international scale at least since the Crimean War, no one seems to have known enough about them to grasp the full implications of their power at home let alone their internationalism.

Thus far, this study supports Edmund Fuller's observation that the munitions maker was "...a type whose existence and reality were generally unsuspected until the popularization of the term merchants of death' after the First World War."[1] George Bernard Shaw anticipated that popularization in *Major Barbara* (1905) when he linked capitalism and war with the figure of the munitions maker. More than likely the conjunction of the ominous prominence of Krupp in Europe and the mysterious activities of Sir Basil Zaharoff had some bearing upon the choice of a cannon king as Shaw's spokesman. Because the full range of the Gospel of St. Andrew Undershaft would take us far afield, it behooves us to limit the discussion of Shaw's complex munitions maker to his political role as a "merchant of death," after which we will look briefly at what Shaw wrote about the origins of the First World War.

If capitalism's natural competitive tendencies led it inevitably

49

to war over sources of raw material and foreign markets, then it
follows that a most important personage either behind the scenes
or on the center-stage of European politics was the man who could
furnish governments with the latest developments in war material
when other nonviolent coercive measures in the bid for economic
supremacy failed. The logical outcome of this set of circumstances
Shaw portrays in *Major Barbara* when he shows that the munitions maker is above the ordinary laws of a nation and the force
behind the government of nations.

Undershaft was not alone in his enterprise, however. Even
Krupp had to deal with his bankers. But Shaw does not give us a
member of a respectable old English banking house. Instead he
conjures up but does not develop to any extent the popular bogey
of the Jewish banker. Here he may have remembered the activities
of the Asiatic Jews who a few years earlier were part of the "Kaffir
Circus" of the London Stock Exchange, that section of the Exchange
with a strong interest in the gold and diamonds of South Africa.[2]
Thus Undershaft is provided with a partner of suitable notoriety.
Stephen Undershaft complains to his mother, Lady Britomart,
about the harassment he had to undergo at school as the son of a
munitions maker who was in league with a Jewish banker: "At
Harrow they called me the Woolwich Infant [an obsolete model of
cannon]. At Cambridge it was the same. A little brute at King's
who was always trying to get up revivals, spoilt my Bible ... by
writing under my name, 'Son and heir to Undershaft and Lazarus,
Death and Destruction Dealers: address, Christendom and
Judea'."[3]

The munitions maker and the Jewish banker are unhampered
by the traditional and legal limits that prescribe the powers of
great statesmen. They are also above the control of the prime
ministers of Europe. Even the molders of public opinion in the
press have little influence upon an enterprise which, as can be said
of Schneider's and Krupp's, assumes the proportion of a state
within a state. Lady Britomart explains all of this to her son
Stephen:

"The True Faith of the Armourer"

It is not only the cannons, but the war loans that Lazarus arranges under cover of giving credit for the cannons. You know, Stephen, it's perfectly scandalous. Those two men, Andrew Undershaft and Lazarus, positively have Europe under their thumbs. That is why your father is able to behave as he does. He is above the law. Do you think Bismarck or Gladstone or Disraeli could have openly defied every social and moral obligation all their lives as your father has? They simply wouldn't have dared. I asked Gladstone to take it up. I asked the Times to take it up. But it was just like asking them to declare war on the Sultan. They wouldn't. They said they couldn't touch him. I believe they were afraid [*Major Barbara*, pp. 221–222].

Not only are the capitalist munitions maker and the banker above the laws of the state, but they are also the powers behind the governments of Europe. Stephen tells his father, who has referred slightingly to the Treasury Bench, that he will not hear the Government of his country insulted. Undershaft replies warmly:

The government of your country! *I* am the government of your country: I, and Lazarus. Do you suppose that you and half a dozen amateurs like you, sitting in a row in that foolish gabble shop, can govern Lazarus? No, my friend: you will do what pays us. You will make war when it suits us, and keep peace when it doesn't. You will find out that trade requires certain measures when we have decided on those measures. When I want anything to keep my dividends up, you will discover that my want is a national need. When other people want something to keep my dividends down, you will call out the police and military. And in return you shall have the support and applause of my newspapers, and the delight of imagining that you are a great statesman! Government of your country! Be off with you, my boy, and play with your caucuses and leading articles and historic parties and great leaders and burning questions and the rest of your toys. *I* am going back to my counting house and pay the piper and call the tune [*Major Barbara*, p. 292].

That speech, making no reference to the sale of cannons, is in essence an indictment of capitalism in general. But in it a munitions maker has said that governments "will make war when it suits" him. That well known outburst goes a long way toward helping to formulate the climate of opinion which would regard the munitions maker solus as the promoter of war. But allowance must be made for dramatic exaggeration, for later in the play Undershaft qualifies his speech to Stephen when he tells Cusins that he has power but none of his own. Cusins asserts that if he inherits Undershaft's gun works, he will do as he pleases, selling or refusing arms as he chooses. The ensuing dialogue indicates that will not be the case:

> UNDERSHAFT: From the moment when you become Andrew Undershaft, you will never do as you please again. Don't come here lusting for power, young man.
> CUSINS: If power were my aim I would not have come here for it. You have no power.
> UNDERSHAFT: None of my own certainly.
> CUSINS: I have more power than you, more will. You do not drive this place: it drives you. And what drives the place?
> UNDERSHAFT: (enigmatically) A will of which I am a part.
> BARBARA: (startled) Father! Do you know what you are saying; or are you laying a snare for my soul?
> CUSINS: Don't listen to his metaphysics, Barbara. The place is driven by the most rascally part of society, the money hunters, the pleasure hunters, the military promotion hunters; and he is their slave.
> UNDERSHAFT: Not necessarily. Remember the Armourer's Faith. I will take orders from a good man as cheerfully as from a bad one [*Major Barbara*, p. 308].

With due heed to Cusins' injunction against Undershaft's "metaphysics" and to continue within a political framework, one is not to take Undershaft's control of the government to mean that all England is his pocket borough, even if popular notions about Krupp hover in the background. Undershaft is the government of England because the Parliament of England is composed of people who have shares in munitions. Before the First World War it was possible to say that "Vickers Ltd., is the stepmother of

"*The True Faith of the Armourer*"

Parliament."[5] At that time the boards of directors of English armaments firms contained a good percentage of Shaw's "English Junkerdom." Retired army and navy officers were commonly representatives because they "knew the ropes," an arrangement that still prevails in present day defense industries in America. In 1911 an English financial journal analyzed the make-up of the directorships of three large armaments firms: Vickers, John Brown, and Armstrong-Whitworth. The statistics revealed that the nobility and titled classes made up the largest proportion of directors. Even a number of bishops served in that capacity.[6] Those were the classes who had most to say about British national security. Just before the war, Philip Snowden did not hesitate to address Parliament with a reformer's zeal on the subject of its members' share-holdings. In the House of Commons he raised the question of MP's holding shares in Vickers and other naval armaments firms: "Now who are the shareholders? It would be too long for me to give more than a very short selection from the list, but I find that honorable members in this House are very largely concerned. Indeed it would be impossible to throw a stone on the benches opposite without hitting a Member who is a shareholder in one or other of these firms." He then listed his colleagues' names and the numbers of their shares.[7]

Thus far, Undershaft has appeared to be a formidable power within his own country. When he announces the internationalist creed of the munitions maker, he certifies himself as a complete "merchant of death" who sells to all who will buy. Patriotism is national; business is international. Lady Britomart puts the moral question about munitions as selling to those "whose cause is right and just" and turning down "foreigners and criminals." Undershaft corrects her by announcing "the true faith of the Armourer": "To give arms to all men who offer an honest price for them, without respect to persons or principles: to aristocrat and republican, to Nihilist and Tsar, to Capitalist and Socialist, to Protestant and Catholic, to burglar and policeman, to black man, white man and yellow man, to all sorts and conditions, all nationalities, all faiths, all follies, all causes and all crimes (*Major Barbara*, p. 307).

In spite of the fact that Undershaft is a complex dramatic creation, not all of whose implications we have looked at, it is tempting
to look for Shaw's source of inspiration. William Manchester is
convinced that *Major Barbara* is a scantily concealed satire on the
Krupps.[8] It is quite probable that Shaw remembered the Krupps
since they had become a household word in munitions by way of
the newspapers very much like Stephen observes about his own
family: "I have hardly ever opened a newspaper in my life without
seeing our name in it. The Undershaft torpedo! The Undershaft
quick firers! The Undershaft ten-inch. The Undershaft disappearing
rampart gun! The Undershaft submarine! and now the Undershaft
aerial battleship!" (*Major Barbara*, p. 221). The newspaper notoriety that also helped along the Krupp name was that variety beloved of the tabloids: the sensational sex scandal leading to the
suicide of Fritz Krupp in the late 1890's after having behaved himself on the isle of Capri as did the Emperor Tiberius nineteen hundred years before. Jules Verne also had a hand in promoting Krupp
steel. He gave the firm unsolicited publicity when Captain Nemo
explained that the engine of his Nautilus was made "by Krupp in
Prussia."[9]

Manchester's comparison cannot be pressed very far, but there
are some interesting coincidences respecting names that he does
not connect with Shaw's play. Bertha Krupp, whom Manchester
sees as Barbara Undershaft, had a younger sister, Barbara, not as
prominent as the first born Bertha. Also St. Barbara is the patron
saint of artillery. In looking for sources, however, we might heed
Shaw's admonition in his "Preface to Major Barbara." He took his
critics to task for the "unpatriotic habit" of assuming that "life and
literature are so poor in these islands that we must go abroad for
all dramatic material that is not common and all ideas that are not
superficial."[10] Were we compelled to take seriously Shaw's injunction and look for a counterpart for Undershaft in the British Isles,
it might well be Sir Basil Zaharoff, "the Mystery Man of Europe,"
Vickers' legendary salesman of death.

If Shaw had a share in popularizing the notion that munitions

makers promoted wars and sold arms to both sides, his personal
views about the impetus behind the First World War were not
quite that simple. For him the causes of that war were rooted
deeply in modern European capitalism. Being a Socialist, he would
not take national sides because to him "them" and "us" were not
separated by the English channel but by class. He did take sides
only out of necessity, as a matter of survival: "I have no ethical
respect for modern Capitalist society, and therefore contemplated
the British, German, and French sections of it with impartial disapproval. I felt as if I were witnessing an engagement between two
pirate fleets, with, however, the very important qualification that
as I and my family and friends were on board British ships I did
not intend the British section to be defeated if I could help it. All the
ensigns were Jolly Rogers; but mine was clearly the one with the
Union Jack in the corner."[11] The war was being fought in the interest of the governing classes or Junkerdom, and "...a Junker was
not a fiend in a spiked helmet but the German equivalent of an
English country gentleman."[12] The English governing classes, both
military and capitalist, sought only to perpetuate "...the organized
legal robbery of the poor; and to that end they would join hands
with the German Junkers against the working classes as readily as
Bismarck joined hands with Thiers to suppress the Commune of
Paris."[13] The rich stood to make much money by the war because
they dealt in things that were in short supply; namely, money and
armaments. Shaw conceded that the interest of the military caste
involved personal danger, "...but the capitalist who has shares in
explosives and cannons and soldiers' boots runs no risk and suffers
no hardship; whilst as to the investor pure and simple, all that
happens to him is that he finds the unearned income obtainable on
Government security larger than ever. Victory to the capitalists
of Europe means that they can not only impose on the enemy a
huge indemnity, but lend him the money to pay for it with whilst
the working classes produce and pay both principal and interest."[14]

The attitude of the Labor party was many stranded; Shaw
shared the sentiments of its most vital section which wanted to

overthrow not only German but all Junkerdom: "...the dynamic section, to which the party owed its formation and which supplies most of its ideas are mainly Socialists and Internationalists who well know that the traditions of the British lion have no future, and that the interests of all proletarians are identical, and, as between one country and another, pacific."[15] Knowing that the Junkers of England and Germany were only seeking to defeat one another in order to establish the winner's brand of Junkerdom, Shaw proposes that the proletarian armies do what Carlyle's Dumdrudges should have done: shoot their officers and go home and start a revolution. He maintains, however, that there is no real danger of that happening but "...it must be frankly mentioned because it or something like it is always a possibility in a defeated conscript army if its commanders push it beyond human endurance when its eyes are opening to the fact that in murdering its neighbors, it is biting off its nose to vex its face, besides riveting the intolerable yoke of Militarism and Junkerdom more tightly than ever on its own neck."[16] In short, Shaw abstracts what he really wrote about the war thus: "Plutocracy makes for war because it offers prizes to Plutocrats; Socialism makes for peace because the interests it serves are international. So as the Socialist side is the democratic side, we had better democratize our diplomacy if we desire peace."[17]

Seven
Germania Delenda Est!

At the outbreak of the First World War, other prominent men of letters saw a need, as public figures, to make a statement justifying England's involvement. Among those, Arnold Bennett and H.G. Wells wrote to rally the British to the colors. Shaw's "common sense about the war" differed in perspective. The Irish dramatist had to hold his tongue in the early weeks of the war owing to his "...Irish capacity for criticizing England with something of the detachment of a foreigner, and perhaps with a certain slightly malicious taste for taking the conceit out of her."[1] Whether considered prejudiced or perverse, Shaw's views were not, as we have seen, those of the British patriot. On the other hand, whatever their private opinions of the many-sidedness of the blame for the commencement of hostilities, Bennett and Wells closed ranks against Germany.

In comparison to Wells, Bennett's statement on liberty is lukewarm for the early days of the war. In this instance at least, he seems to lack the spontaneity that is the temperamental requisite of the natural propagandist. Nevertheless, he brought the munitions maker under scrutiny. Bennett saw the German military caste, the Kaiser and the Krupps as responsible for the glorification of German arms: "The best qualities of the race were turned to evil, and its worst quality, a certain maladroit arrogance, was appealed to. The army and God were more and more, the staple subjects of official speeches, and the result has been a national obsession of such completeness that ladies have to make room for the swagger of Prussian officers three abreast on the pavements of enlightened

German cities, and the Kaiser himself has closely fraternized with the sinister Krupp family."[2] Like Shaw, who "...did not want Hohenzollerism to win because it was evident that in spite of its monarchial idealism, it could not control Militarism and was in effect controlled by it,"[3] Bennett believed that the German military caste had manipulated the Kaiser into war; and Krupp, in a show of patriotism prepared a smoother way through Belgium: "On the whole the caste must have been too much for the Kaiser; nevertheless the Kaiser who would often very annoyingly flirt with peace, had always to be managed, and the murder of a Teutonic heir-apparent enabled the caste to get at him on his dynastic side.... And the characteristic political simplicity of the caste saw good signs everywhere.... Krupp had deliberately broken his contract with the Belgian Government for big guns, and Belgian forts therefore could not hold out...."[4]

Considering the volume of his writings on the war, Shaw hardly mentions the Krupps. The name appears only on two occasions when he analyzes the war fever of "British Bulldog Jingoism." The two instances are worth a glance because they reveal the degree to which the name Krupp inspired fear and suspicion amid the hysteria of war. In one case, after the Archbishop of York had stated that his personal impression of the Kaiser was that he did not seem fiendish, the British jingoes immediately raised a howl that "...the Archbishop had sold his country to the Germans and was longing to see York Cathedral bombarded by Krupp guns, and the eyes and hands of the inhabitants gouged out and chopped off by intoxicated Uhlans whilst the Archbishop roystered with the Crown Prince in the episcopal palace."[5] The other reference to Krupp was made in connection with Shaw's account of the first time he heard the demagoguery of Horatio Bottomley, editor of the popular jingo paper *John Bull*, the theme of which was the betrayal of England from within:

> I have seldom been so surprised as when I had the pleasure last autumn of hearing Mr. Horatio Bottomley speak for the first

time. I expected to hear — he had led me to expect to hear — a fire-eater. Never has a public man done himself a more wanton injustice. Had the British Army heard his address every soldier would have fled weeping from the field. No lachrymatory shells ever discharged from a German gun could have produced such a sense of despair. Poor, lost, duped, silly England, conducting Herr Krupp's relatives through her dockyards and arsenals, and explaining all her secrets to them, whilst Mr. Bottomley and his friend Edward VII vainly implored their country to beware, was depicted with a grieving sentimentality more depressing than the influenza.[6]

Possessing neither Bennett's tepidity nor Shaw's Irish detachment, H.G. Wells saw the necessity of galvanizing his country men into a fighting attitude. And in September, 1914, one month after the march into Belgium, with the news of Belgian atrocities still in the air and Britain committed to fight for Belgium, Wells published a collection of eleven articles, titled with the slogan, *The War That Will End War*. In that shilling pamphlet meant for mass circulation, Wells can be seen as the very likely source for the wide circulation of the idea that munitions makers, with their insidious power over governments were the real warmakers. The Kaiser and Krupp, address Berlin and Essen, were partners in a return to barbarism.

Outlining why Britain went to war, Wells warms up to his subject by affirming the need to "...destroy an evil system of government and the mental and material corruption that has got hold of the German imagination and taken possession of German life."[7] Germany, once the home of Goethe, is now both externally and internally corrupt. The armaments octopus has presided over the land as head of a state within a state and has paralyzed the intellectual life of Germany:

> The man [the Kaiser] who preaches cynicism in his own business transactions had better keep a detective and a cash register for his clerks; and it is the most natural thing in the world to find that this system which is so outwardly vile, is also inwardly

rotten. Beside the Kaiser stands the firm of Krupp, a second head
to the state; on the very steps of the throne is the armaments
trust, that organized scoundrelism which has, in its relentless
propaganda for profit, mined all the security of civilization,
brought up and dominated a Press, ruled a national literature and
corrupted universities [*End War*, p. 10].

Heady with the victories of the sixties against Denmark and Austria
and in the seventies against France, the German people, in many
ways "the most civilized in the world," succumbed to "a propaganda
of national vanity and national ambition," which was exploited by
the weapons industry:

It [propaganda] was organized by a stupidly forceful statesman, it was fostered by folly upon the throne. It was guarded
from wholesome criticism by an intolerant censorship. It never
gave sanity a chance. A certain patriotic sentimentality lent itself only too readily to the suggestion of the flatterer, and so there
grew up this monstrous trade in weapons. German patriotism
became an "interest," the greatest of "interests." It developed a vast
advertisement propaganda. It subsidized Navy Leagues and
Aerial Leagues, threatening the world. Mankind, we saw too late,
had been guilty of an incalculable folly in permitting private men
to make a profit out of the dreadful preparations of war. But the
evil was started; the German imagination was captured and en-
slaved [*End War*, pp. 10–11].

One division of Wells' pamphlet dissects the character and
activities of the symbolic Mr. Maximilian Craft. He stands as the
secret agent of the international armaments trade, the spirit that encouraged all countries to be prepared against their neighbors.
(Krupp had sold arms to over fifty countries by the time of the
First World War. Even little Andorra had purchased a cannon
which could not be tested within her borders because the range of
the gun was greater than the farthest distance between her fron-
tiers.) Craft is not a born but a naturalized Englishman, originally
a Kraft from Germany. Here Wells plays upon the meanings of the

name in the two languages, "Kraft" meaning "power" which this nominal English citizen seeks to further in England by "craft." This man waves the Union Jack "...as if St. George was his father" and advises the English on the conduct of the war, his wisdom having been acquired from "those professors of Welt Politick who have guided the German mind to its present magnificent display of shrewd triumphant statecraft" (*End War*, p. 30). For Craft wars are to be waged employing any stratagem, device, or scheme, no matter whether it be something "nationally dishonest and disgraceful."

The spirit of Kraft is not native to England, however; and England wants no part of him and his friends, the munitions makers:

> Now let us English make it clear, once and for all, to the Krafts and other kindred patriotic gentlemen from abroad who are showing us the really artful way of doing things. Into this war we have gone with clean hands—to end the reign of brutal and artful internationalism for ever.... We mean to fight this war to its very finish, and that finish we are absolutely resolved must be the end of Kraftism in the world. And we will come out of this war with hands as clean as they are now, unstained by any dirty tricks in field or council chamber, neutralities respected and treaties kept. Then we will reckon once for all with Kraft and with his friends and supporters, the private dealers in armaments, and with all this monstrous, stupid brood of villainy that has brought this vast catastrophe upon the world [*End War*, p. 34].

Craft wants to be on hand when this war is over so that he can set up all the conditions existing prior to the war which will mean business as usual for the armaments firms. That, Wells informs us, is known as modern diplomacy; but it will not be so:

> He betrays at times a remarkable persuasion that at the final settling up of things he will make himself invaluable to us. At diplomacy he knows he shines.... Finish the fighting, and then leave it to him. He really believes the born English will.... This

war is not going to end in diplomacy; it is going to end diplomacy.... At the end there will be no Conference of Europe on the old lines at all but a Conference of the World.... And it will make a peace that will put an end to Kraft and the spirit of Kraft and Kraftism and the private armament firms behind him for ever more.... When we fight Berlin, Kraft, we fight you.... An absolute end to you [*End War*, pp. 35–36].

In another division of his pamphlet, Wells focusses upon the munitions makers to recommend "the most necessary measures in the world." *Porro unum est necessarium*. Considered an unworkable idea up to the time of the war, the destruction of the private armaments industry can now be accomplished:

In this smash-up of empires and diplomacy, this utter disaster of international politics, certain things which would have seemed ridiculously Utopian a few weeks ago have suddenly become reasonable and practicable. One of these, a thing that would have seemed fantastic until the very moment when we joined issue with Germany and which now may be regarded as a sober possibility, is the absolute abolition throughout the world of the manufacture of weapons for private gain. Whatever may be said of the practicability of national disarmament, there can be no dispute not merely of the possibility but of the supreme necessity of ending for ever the days of private profit in the instruments of death. That is the real enemy. That is the evil thing at the very center of this trouble [*End War*, p. 37].

Wells summarizes the far reaching sinister and malevolent organizational operations of Kruppism:

At the very core of all this evil that has burst at last in world disaster lies this Kruppism, this sordid enormous trade in the instruments of death. It is the closest, most gigantic organisation in the world. Time after time this huge business, with its bought newspapers, its paid spies, its agents, its shareholders, its insane sympathizers, its vast ramification of open and concealed associates, has defeated attempts at pacification, has piled the heap of explosive material higher and higher — the heap that has toppled at last into this bloody welter in Belgium, in which the lives of four great nations are now being torn and tormented and slaughtered and wasted beyond counting, beyond imagining [*End War*, pp. 37–38].

While the world had readied for war following the ancient adage, *si vis pacem, pare bellum* — if you desire peace, prepare for war, Krupp sales were in the ascendant. Now that armed peace has become armed conflict, the age old precept proves itself to be bankrupt, thus adding another reason for the need to bring Kruppism to an end:

> So long as the unstable peace endured, so long as the Emperor of the Germans and the Krupp concern and the vanities of Prussia hung together, threatening but not assailing the peace of the world, so long as we could dream of holding off the crush and saving lives, so long was it impossible to bring this business to an end. It was still possible to argue that to prepare for war was the way to keep the peace. But now everyone knows better. The war has come. Preparation has exploded. Outrageous plunder has passed into outrageous bloodshed. All Europe is in revolt against this evil system. There is no going back now to peace.... Out of it must come one universal resolve: that this iniquity must be plucked out by the roots. Whatever follies still lie ahead for mankind this folly at least must end. There must be no more buying and selling guns and warships and war-machines. There must be no more gain in arms. Kings and Kaisers must cease to be the commercial travellers of monstrous armaments concerns. With the *Goeben* the Kaiser has made his last sale. Whatever arms the nations think they need they must make for themselves and give to their own subjects. Beyond that there must be no making of weapons in the earth [*End War*, pp. 38–39].

All the world knows the evident connection between the Kaiser and Krupp. Destroy the Kaiser and you destroy Krupp. Therefore, Berlin *delenda est:*

> I do not need to argue what is manifest, what every German knows, what every intelligent man in the world knows. The

Krupp concern and the tawdry Imperialism of Berlin are linked like thief and receiver; the hands of the German princes are dirty with the trade. All over the world statecraft and royalty have been approached by these vast firms, but it is Berlin that the intolerable pressure to arm and still to arm has come, it is at Berlin alone that this evil can be grappled and killed. It was useless to dream of disarmament while these people could still go on making their material uncontrolled, waiting for the moment of national passion, feeding the national mind with fears and suspicions through their subsidised Press.... We can at least deal with Krupps and the kindred firms throughout the world as one general problem, one world-wide accessible evil [*End War*, pp. 39–40].

Wells' solution to the problem of the private trade in armaments is to nationalize the industry so that the State will control the making of weapons:

Let me set out the suggestion very plainly. All the plant for the making of war material throughout the world must be taken over by the government of the state in which it exists; every gun factory, every rifle factory, every dockyard for the building of warships. It may be necessary to compensate the shareholders more or less completely; there may have to be a war indemnity to provide for that, but that is a question of detail. The thing is the conversion everywhere of arms-making into a State monopoly, so that nowhere shall there be a ha-porth of avoidable private gain in it. Then, and only then, will it become possible to arrange for the gradual dismantling of this industry which is destroying humanity, and the reduction of the armed forces of the world to reasonable dimensions [*End War*, p. 41].

Though it seemed a Utopian idea even to him, Wells was a believer in world wide governmental control over weapons of calibres both large and small: "I would carry this suppression down even to the restriction of the manufacture and sale of every sort of gun, pistol, and explosive. They should be made only in Government workshops and sold only in Government shops; there should not be a single rifle, not a Browning pistol, unregistered, unrecorded, and untraceable in the world. But that may be a counsel of perfection" (*End War*, p. 41). Most important, however, is the need to get rid of the big hardware of war.

But the world cannot talk about peace and disarmament without getting rid of the travelling salesman of armaments. Even with him gone, though, Wells does not advocate total disarmament as long as any one country remains chauvinistic:

> With this corruption cleared out of the way, with the armaments commercial traveller flung down the back-stairs he has haunted for so long—and flung so hard that we will be incapacitated for ever—it will become possible to consider a scheme for the establishment of the peace of the world. Until that is done any such scheme will remain an idle dream. But him disposed of, the way is open for the association of armed nations, determined to stamp out at once every recrudescence of aggressive war. They will not be totally disarmed Powers. It is no good to disarm while any one single Power is still in love with the dream of military glory [*End War*, pp. 41–42].

After the war, with courage and honesty, the nations of the world can establish a world organization, a "Peace League," for the control of armaments. But first the trade in arms must be extinguished absolutely; and the sea made a neutral ground with nations no longer vying for its control: "And the world will be ripe, too, for the banishment of the private industry in armaments and all the vast corruption that entails from the earth forever. It is possible now to make an end to Kruppism. It may never be possible again" (*End War*, p. 62). First *Germania delenda est*, for "the fate of the world under triumphant Prussianism and Kruppism for the next two hundred years is not worth discussing" (*End War*, p. 44). After the war, the boundaries of European nations will be adjusted to end tensions. Disputes over boundaries have "wasted the forces of civilization (and made the fortunes of the Krupp family) in the last forty years" (*End War*, pp. 49–50).

As Cato, after he saw the resources of Carthage, never made a speech in Rome without ending it with the phrase, *Carthago delenda est,* so Wells repeatedly asserts that Kaiserism and Kruppism must be destroyed. It is that "evil" which this, "the greatest of all wars," will crush: "There will be no more Kaisers, there will be no more Krupps we are resolved. That foolery shall end!" (*End War*, p. 12). Lovers of peace will see the "...ending for good and all of the blood and iron superstition, of Krupp, of flag-waving Teutonic Kiplingism, and all that sham efficiency that centres in Berlin. Never was war so righteous as war against Germany now. Never has any state in the world so clamoured for punishment" (*End War*, p. 14).

To allay the Liberals' fear of Tsarist Russia, Wells argues that Russia is not as dangerous as the "Kaiser-Krupp power we fight to the finish" (*End War*, p. 71). If there will be trouble from Russia, it is not pressing. On the other hand, "the danger of a Krupp-cum-Kaiser dominance of the whole world ... is immediate. Defeat, or even a partial victory for the Allies, means nothing less than that" (*End War*, p. 72).

Before long it becomes clear that with his continual references to the radical evil of "Kruppism," Wells is writing both war propaganda and propaganda against war, trying to fix in the English mind the title of his pamphlet as a slogan or catch-phrase which will carry them through the difficult time ahead. The final section of the pamphlet is called "The War of the Mind." Wells' propaganda transcends the needs of one people at war; he proposes to eradicate the idea of war through leaflets and tracts written in many languages. Above all, he disdains the economic argument against war — that it does not pay. Instead of figures of the kind that Norman Angell, economist and worker for international peace, would argue from, Wells wants photos of war's casualties juxtaposed to those of Germans responsible: "...photographs of the Kaiser in his glory at a review, and photographs of the long, unintelligent sidelong face of the Crown Prince, his son, photographs of that original Krupp taking his pleasures at Capri; and to set beside these, photographs pitilessly showing men killed and horribly torn apart upon the battlefield, and men crippled and women and men murdered, and homes burnt and, to the verge of indecency, all the peculiar filthiness of war" (*End War*, p. 93).

By virtue of its medium, Shaw's *Major Barbara* was written for a select audience. Moreover, what was the play about? The arms industry? The "crime" of poverty? "Crosstianity?" That ambiguity, along with Shaw's wit, makes the play perpetually fascinating. On the other hand, nine years later with Europe in flames, Wells strenuously avoided ambiguity in his assault on the munitions industry. His shilling pamphlet was meant for mass circulation. The complex political arrangements which brought on the war had to be reduced to a readily identifiable quantity. That simplification was achieved by anthropomorphising the causes of the First World War into the twin symbols of Kaiser and Krupp.

Eight
The Men Who Marched Away

A dozen years after the Armistice a wave of anti-war sentiment swept through England. Although it is difficult to gauge the extent of its influence, a concentration of fiction, drama, and memoirs about the war also emerged in the last two years of the twenties. Not that there had not been earlier renderings of war experience. C.E. Montague, who dyed his graying hair in order to enlist and who, on one occasion, escorted Shaw on a visit to the front, published his *Disenchantment* in 1922. Ford Madox Ford's Tietjens tetralogy was written between 1924 and 1928. But Montague and Ford were both older men at the time of the war, and it seems that younger writers needed at least ten years to assimilate their war experience. In 1928 there appeared Edmund Blunden's *Undertones of War* and R.C. Sherriff's *Journey's End*; in 1929, Richard Aldington's *Death of a Hero*, Erich Maria Remarque's *All Quiet on the Western Front* (translated, and put on the screen a year later), and Robert Graves' *Goodbye to All That*; in 1930, Siegfried Sassoon's *Memoirs of an Infantry Officer* and Frederic Manning's *Her Privates We* by Private 19022. All expressed the futility, incompetence, and victimization of the First World War.[1]

In order to see another sort of perspective on the causes of war, it is fruitful to inquire into that concentrated stir of literary activity at the end of the twenties. Up to this point, we have been examining the opinions of men of letters and prominent historical figures who have discussed the causes of war as they perceived them from intellectual and moral conviction. Now we can regard the points of view of literary men who were participants in the war, whose consciousness was not that of the philosophically detached noncombatant but shaped by the combination of personal background and individual physical circumstances each found himself in after he put on a uniform. Referring to private soldiers in a way applicable to both officers and men, Frederic Manning wrote in 1930: "Their judgments were necessarily partial and prejudiced; but prejudices and partialities provide most of the driving power of life. It is better to allow them to cancel each other, than to attempt to strike an average between them.... [M]y concern has been mainly with the anonymous ranks, whose opinion, often mere surmise and ill informed, but real and true for them, I have tried to represent faithfully."[2] Were those partialities personal or political? We need to cast a glance at the degree of awareness of the causes of war shown by the men who wrote about life in the trenches. It would be better not to attempt, at this point at least, to strike an average of those impressions.

Graves' *Goodbye to All That*, Sherriff's *Journey's End*, and Blunden's *Undertones of War* are examples of the purely personal response to the war. Except for a reference to defective ammunition made in America, we get very little out of Graves about war profiteering or the political causes of war. The general impression that emanates from Graves' autobiography is that on the battleground of France are two teams, one Allied and the other German. The participants have a profound respect for a worthy opponent and the player's not so well disguised contempt for the cheering spectators and, we may add, for the local hawkers of food.[3] In *Journey's End* there is no debate about the causes of war. The play is a drama of personal heroism and the stresses of trench life among a group of English officers. Sheriff's characters dwell, too, with some relish upon such immediate soldierly concerns as the next meal's possibilities. From *Undertones of War* we hear again that the name Krupp was synonymous with artillery. Blunden mentions a German artillery bombardment and his company doctor's indifference to "such annoyances as Krupp."[4]

Aldington's *Death of a Hero*, charitable to capitalists and governments, is *sui generis* in proposing overpopulation as the prime mover of war. Half asleep in a troop train, George Winterbourne ponders the origins of war:

> What's really the cause of wars, of this War? Oh, you can't say one cause; there are many. The Socialists are silly fanatics when they say it's the wicked capitalists. I don't believe the capitalists wanted a war—they stand to lose too much in the disturbance. And I don't believe the wretched governments really wanted it—they were shoved on by great forces they're too timid and too unintelligent to control. It's the superstition of more babies and more bread.... There may be commercial motives behind this War, jolly short-sighted ones—they've already lost more than they can possibly gain. No, this is fundamentally a population War—bread and babies, babies and bread.[5]

The view of the common soldier written down by one of them, the view unfortunately so unaccounted for in the literature of the First World War, appears in Remarque's *All Quiet on the Western Front* and Manning's *Her Privates We*. Toward the end of the war, Remarque's Paul Baumer details, to use the phraseology of R.E. Lee's last general order, the "overwhelming numbers and resources" of the English and Americans in comparison with the exhaustion of the Germans. Someone back in Germany has profited handsomely, he wearily accuses: "But we are emaciated and starved. Our food is so bad and mixed up with so much substitute stuff that it makes us ill. The factory owners in Germany have grown wealthy; —dysentery dissolves our bowels."[6]

The "prejudices and partialities" of Manning's "anonymous ranks" are shaped by their preference for the knowledge of the senses. To the common soldier in Manning's book, acquaintance with the war profiteer is confined to direct experience with members of his class. Two privates tell the story of their fight in a pub with a miner who boasted that he did not work longer than a total of eight hours for his fist full of week's wages and who expressed a desire that the war last forever. One listener generalizes about such civilian fellow workingmen: "It's them chaps what are always on the make, an' don't care 'ow they make it, as causes 'arf the wars. Them's the bloody cowards" (*Privates*, pp. 277–279). Manning's common soldiers exhibit no sense of being exploited by a higher class. One enlisted man expresses a British Bulldog or, better labelled, an anti-Dumdrudge opinion: "I'm not fighting for a lot of bloody civvies.... I'm fightin' for myself an' me own folk. It's all bloody fine sayin', 'let them as made the war fight it.' 'Twere Germany made the war" (*Privates*, p. 275).

Among the English soldier writers publishing in the late twenties, Siegfried Sassoon was the most politically aware, so much so that during the war he wrote a letter of protest to the military authorities. *Memoirs of an Infantry Officer* records the beginning of his change of outlook when he describes the effect of seeing in France a dead soldier's hands uplifted toward Heaven: "But I can remember a pair of hands (nationality unknown) which protruded from the soaked ashen soil like the roots of a tree turned upside down; one hand seemed to be pointing at the sky with an accusing gesture. Each time I passed that place the protest of those fingers became more expressive of an appeal to God in defiance of those who made the War. Who made the War? I laughed hysterically as the thought passed through my mud-stained mind."[7] For Sassoon, England had let down the English soldiers by permitting the war to continue unnecessarily. In a statement to his superior officers, he listed his objections to the war: "Something must be put on paper ... and I re-scrutinized the rough notes I'd been making. Fighting men are victims of conspiracy among (a) politicians; (b) military caste; (c) people who are making money out of the War.... I am not a conscientious objector. I am a soldier who believes he is acting on behalf of soldiers.... I am making this statement as an act of willful defiance of military authority because I believe that the War is being deliberately prolonged by those who have the power to end it" (*Memoirs*, pp. 277–278).

Particularly disconcerting to Sassoon was the war profiteer. The comparison to the best examples of humanity he had seen at the front was inescapable. He believed that military men were capable of the kind of nobility Ruskin had seen in them: "I thought of the typical Flintshire Fusilier at his best, and the vast anonymity of courage and cheerfulness which he represented as he sat in a front line trench cleaning his mess-tin. How could one connect him with the gross profiteer whom I'd overheard in a railway carriage remarking to an equally repulsive companion that if the War lasted another eighteen months he'd be able to retire from business?" (*Memoirs*, p. 277). The professional soldier was happy to be in France in order to avoid seeing examples of the dishonesty of men making money out of the war. Sassoon describes a regular army major he met who had served from the time of the Boer War and had been seriously wounded at Ypres, "...but in spite of this he was a resolute optimist and was delighted to be back in France.... England, he said, was no place for an honest man; the sight of all those dirty dogs swindling the Government made him sick" (*Memoirs*, p. 170).

When on leave Sassoon made it a point to go out to public places and observe the newly prosperous. Some members of this new order of men he saw with a fellow officer at the Olympic Hotel in Liverpool:

> "Fivers" melted very rapidly at the Olympic, and many of them were being melted by people whose share in the national effort was difficult to diagnose. In the dining room I began to observe that some noncombatants were doing themselves pretty well out of the War. They were people whose faces lacked nobility, as they ordered lobsters and selected colossal cigars. I remember drawing Durley's attention to some such group when he dined with me.... I said that I supposed they must be profiteers. For a moment Durley regarded them with unspeculative eyes, but he made no comment; if he found them incredible, it wasn't surprising; both his brothers had been killed in action and his sense of humour had suffered in proportion [*Memoirs*, p. 150].

After writing his letter of protest, Sassoon worked to keep his resolve from flagging. From time to time, he would bolster his spirits by seeking out in public places those who profited from the war: "I was existing in a world of my own (in which I tried to keep my courage up to protest-pitch). From the visible world I sought evidence which could aggravate my quarrel with acquiescent patriotism. Evidences of civilian callousness and complacency were plentiful, for the thriftless license of war-time behavior was an unavoidable spectacle, especially in the Savoy Hotel Grill Room which I visited more than once in my anxiety to reassure myself of the existence of bloated profiteers and uniformed jacks in office" (*Memoirs*, pp. 280–281).

Sassoon's acquaintance with profiteers is confined to his direct observation of watching them feed and his conclusions are drawn from that limited experience. Perhaps the most eloquent and informed statement against profiteering was not written until 1933 by Guy Chapman, who was sufficiently alienated by its cultural implications that he was unwilling to go back to England after the Armistice and volunteered instead to serve in the Army of Occupation: "Our civilization was being torn to pieces before our eyes. England was said to be a country fit only for profiteers to live in. *Esti de ou pros Lakedaemonious hemeen o agon.* Many of us were growing bitter. We had no longer the desire to go back. Isn't there a fairy tale about two countries held together by a hair and when that broke, they fled apart? England had vanished over the horizon of the mind. I did not want to see it."[8] The old values of prewar England were gone. The English cared only for money and particularly excess profit. Chapman also hints at international dealings with the enemy:

> As the war trailed its body across France, slimming the landscape, so too it tainted civilian life. London seemed poorer and yet more raffish. Its dignity was melting under the strain. It had become corrupted. There was a feeling of hostility growing up between the soldiers abroad and the civilians and soldiers at home; the good-timers, the army abroad thought them, profiteering, drinking, debauching the women. There were ugly tales of money-making in coal, wheat, wool, tea, and other necessities far above legitimate profit, stories of farmers' profits, of breweries'

> winnings. The 1914 values had gone bad, and instead, the English were learning to respect one thing only, money, and easy money by preference. It was better in France. There a man was valued rather for what he was than what he had achieved. One found germinating in one's mind the seed of a hatred for those home-keeping English. One might have recalled that it is the habit of the English from the days of Marlborough to trade with the enemy. Was not Napoleon's army shod by England? But the habitual rapacity of man seemed no excuse when it was not a dynasty but the whole nation in arms (*Prodigality*, pp. 112–113).[9]

We would be remiss to pass from the group of English soldier writers who published in the late twenties without mentioning the work of some of their predecessors writing in the decade from 1918 to 1928. As was noted before, the writers of that decade chanced to belong to an older generation whose assimilation of the war experience may have come earlier owing to their maturity at the time of the First World War. Remarque points to that phenomenon in *All Quiet* when he notes the bewilderment of the young soldier straight out of secondary school into the trenches who had no dream of the past to sustain him, no wife, no children, no occupation, no identity before the war to which to return if he survived with his life. In his later fiction that younger generation continues to drift through the postwar years and are appropriately characterized by the title of one of his novels, *Flotsam*. The stability of the older generation reveals itself in the distance they are able to put between themselves and the war. It may be that after having lost the feeling of immortality of youth, they had suffered in other ways and thus looked upon the agony of war as another test of endurance that life exacts.

Rose Macaulay, born in 1881, referred to the First World War as a capitalist's war in *Potterism* (1920), but, all the same, a war that had to be won. The Potters were considered profiteers by a returning veteran, but they are called that in a larger sense than that of war profiteer. They are the ruling classes, the grabbers who exploit not only in wartime. Moving even further from the specific association with excess earnings from war contracts, Rose Macaulay insisted that we are all exploiters: "The war profiteers exploited the war.... We all exploit other people — use their affection, their dependence on us, their needs and their sins, for our own ends."[10]

Ford Madox Ford was fifty-two years old when he published *No More Parades* in 1925. In that novel he declared that, as a writer on active service in the war, he felt an obligation to help bring about through his writings "...such a state of mind as should end wars as possibilities." But how to do it was the artist's rub. If the writer piles horror upon horror or heroic action upon heroic action, the effect is the same. In either case, overstatement would ultimately lead to indifference on the part of the reader. Ford chose instead to try to evoke the worry that plagued the men in France: "The never-ending sense of worry, in fact, far surpassed any of the 'exigencies of troops actually in contact with enemy forces,' and that applied not merely to the bases but the whole field of military operations. Unceasing worry!" *No More Parades* purports to be a record of the opinions of English soldiery who felt that they had been let down by those in control. Whether the opinions were justified, Ford will not say. Extremely sensitive to having been identified with his characters, he disclaims any connection with what the soldiers thought about their leadership, saying that he has never had any opinion on the "public matters here discussed."[11]

If Ford himself is not critical of the quality of English military leadership in France, neither is C.E. Montague entirely condemnatory of the war profiteer. Montague was forty-seven years old when in 1914 he began his five years of service in the British Army. Whether it was a function of his mature years or his first hand knowledge of military supplies and equipment, he displayed an amused tolerance toward the profiteer, a slightly sardonic resignation about what some men were capable of under temptation of gain. The war materiel was expensive, but at least it was not shoddy or ersatz as Remarque records. Even in their war profiteering, the English did not go to extremes:

> In their vices as well as their virtues the English preserve a distinguished moderation.... So, when the war with its great opportunities came, we were but temperately robbed by our own birds of prey. Makers of munitions made mighty fortunes out of our peril. Still every British soldier did have a rifle, at any rate, when he went to the front. I have watched a twelve-inch gun fire, in action, fifteen of its great bales or barrels of high explosives, fifteen running, and only three of the fifteen costly packages failed to explode duly on its arrival beyond. Vendors of soldiers' clothes and boots acquired from us the wealth which dazzles us all in these days of our poverty. They knew how to charge; they made hay with a will while the blessed suns of 1914-18 were high in the heavens. Still, nearly all the tunics made in that day of temptation did hold together; none of the boots as far as I know or heard tell, was made of brown paper. "He that maketh haste to be rich shall not be innocent." Still, there is reason in everything. *"Meden agan,"* as the Greeks said — temperance in all things even in robbery, even in patriotism and personal honour. Our profiteers did not bid Satan get him behind them; but they did ask him to stand a little to one side.[12]

If, for the sake of comparison, we look at several writers who served in the armies of other nations, we discover that general conclusions about their awareness of who made the war are no easier to draw than is the case among English literary men. Arnold Zweig does not take up the origins of the war in *The Case of Sergeant Grischa* (1928). The hapless Grischa, an escaped Russian prisoner of war, is shot as a spy as a result of the impersonal machinery of German military officialdom. Jaroslav Hasek declines to introduce serious discussion about the war in *The Good Soldier Schweik* (1930) because it is not in keeping with the spirit of his satire on the Austrian army. On an occasion when a schoolmaster-turned-soldier begins to explain the origins of war, his fantastic account attributing war to sunspots is cut short, thus leaving the field to Schweik, the ingenu, to launch into a chain of associative digressions that is characteristic of him, a device that allows both for comic possibilities and a way of sidestepping the war:

There are scientists who say that war is due to sun spots. Whenever a sun spot makes its appearance, some disaster or other is
bound to happen. The capture of Carthage — "
  "Oh, you shut up and keep all that scientific muck to yourself,"
interposed the corporal. "The best thing you can do is to sweep
the room out. You're on fatigue to-day. We don't care damn-all
about sun spots. I wouldn't take a dozen of 'em, not if they was
offered to me as a gift."
  "These here sun spots are jolly important," intervened Schweik.
Once there was a sun spot and on that very same day I got an
awful walloping in a pub.... Ever since then, if I have to go anywhere, I always have a look in the papers to see whether another
spot's been spotted, so to speak. And if it has, why, I don't go
nowhere, no, not me, thanks all the same. When that volcano
blew up the whole island of Martinique, there was a professor
chap wrote in the *Narodni Politika* that he had been warning
readers for quite a long time about a big sun spot. Only the
Narodni Politika didn't get to the island in time, and so the
people on the island got done in."[13]

Although the major figures of Hemingway's *A Farewell to
Arms* (1929) are reticent about the causes of war, a few of the minor
Italian characters talk politics early in the novel. Stupidity, not
profit, is given as the reason for Italy's involvement in the war,
maintains Passini, whose death a few pages later seems, like Mer-
cutio's, a waste of dramatic possibilities:

  We think. We read. We are not peasants. We are mechanics.
  But even then the peasants know better than to believe in a war.
  Everybody hates this war.
    There is a class that controls a country that is stupid and does
  not realize anything and never can. That is why we have this
  war.
    Also they make money out of it.
    "Most of them don't" said Passini. "They are too stupid. They
  do it for nothing. For stupidity."[14]

Looking back to his own part in the First World War, the dis-
tinguished American historian, William L. Langer, a member of

one of the chemical warfare companies, recalls that Americans were anxious to get to the front not so much out of ideological conviction but out of a hankering for adventure:

> What strikes me most, I think, is the constant reference to the eagerness of the men to get to France and above all to reach the front. One would think that, after almost four years of war, after the most detailed and realistic accounts of the murderous fighting on the Somme and around Verdun, to say nothing of the day-to-day agony of trench warfare, it would have been all but impossible to get anyone to serve without duress. But it was not so. We and many thousands of others volunteered. Perhaps we were offended by the arrogance of the German U-boat campaign and convinced that Kaiserism must be smashed, once for all. Possibly we already felt that, in the American interest Western democracy must not be allowed to go under. But I doubt it. I can hardly remember a single instance of serious discussion of American policy or of larger war issues. We men, most of us young, were simply fascinated by the prospect of adventure and heroism. Most of us, I think, had the feeling that life, if we survived, would run in the familiar, routine channel. Here was our one great chance for excitement and risk. We could not afford to pass it up.[15]

In his account of the Amsterdam Anti-War Congress of 1932 in *The Long Weekend*, Robert Graves mentions the presence of Henri Barbusse. A writer whose pacificism eventually led him to Communism, Barbusse is the most politically conscious of this group of international soldier writers. In *Under Fire* (1916) Barbusse assigns the reason for war to the combination of militarism, capitalism, conservatism, and nationalism present in all countries. The "gilded men," who are set up as privileged by the multitude and who "will suddenly weigh down the scales of justice when they think they see great profit to gain," are, together with the "warrior class," advocates of war:

> There is not only the prodigious opposition of interested parties — financiers, speculators great and small, armour-plated in their banks and houses, who live on war and live in peace during

war, with their brows stubbornly set upon a secret doctrine and their faces shut up like safes.

> There are those who admire the exchange of flashing blows, who hail like women the bright colours of uniforms; those whom military music and the martial ballads poured upon the public intoxicate as with brandy; the dizzy-brained, the feeble-minded, the superstitious, the savages.[16]

Some do not see war as an unpredictable force for change in the long run but only as a means to prevent it. They fight to preserve the past and the present: "There are those who bury themselves in the past, on whose lips are the sayings only of bygone days, the traditionalists for whom an injustice has legal force because it is perpetuated, who aspire to be guided by the dead, who strive to subordinate progress and the future and all their palpitating passion to the realm of ghosts and nursery-tales." Others exalt the national will as absolute truth: "They pervert the most admirable of moral principles. How many are the crimes of which they have made virtues merely by dowering them with the word 'national'? They distort even truth itself. For the truth which is eternally the same they substitute each their national truth. So many nations, so many truths; and thus they falsify and twist the truth." Addressing his critique of war to French soldiers, Barbusse employs the Dumdrudge argument, identifying the enemy not by nationality but by class: "All those people are your enemies.... They are your enemies as much as those German soldiers are today who prostrate themselves here between you in the mud, who are only poor dupes, hatefully deceived and brutalized, domestic beasts" (*Under Fire*, p. 340).

What can we glean about the origins of war from this diversity of partial portraits of it by literary men who marched away? Under what generalization can we subsume their experience? It seems that the strongest impression we gain from that survey is that the greater part of even the most articulate of fighting men in the First World War were not inclined to be philosophers of war in the sense that they thought about it politically. The combatants' experiences were sufficiently engrossing that larger issues were subordinated to both their fascination and the practical necessity of attending to survival in the face of immediate danger for self and comrades.

Perhaps the most significant factor which inhibited the development of a sophisticated political outlook among many of the English men at war was the polarization resulting from their experience. "Them" and "us" was an obvious division to the unreflecting jingo. To the Socialist-internationalist-pacifist, those two opposing forces were the governing classes of all nations set against the exploited governed. To officers and men in the trenches, that dichotomy became soldier on one side and civilian on the other. Not that the soldier was unaware of the economic gains many civilians were making back home at his expense, but what isolated him from the civilian was the incomprehensibility of his experience to any one other than a comrade in arms, and added to that, his bafflement at the civilian's idea of what was going on in France. There were two wars being fought, one in the trenches and an extraordinarily different war in the minds of the civilians. One of Manning's privates on leave thought that it was futile to explain the difference to a voluble civilian: "They don't care a rap what 'appens to 'us'ns, so long as they can keep a 'ole skin. Say they be ready to make any sacrifice; but we're the bloody sacrifice. You never seed such a windy lot; an' bloodthirsty ain't the word for it. They've all gone potty. You'd think your best friends wouldn't be satisfied until they'd seed your name on the roll of honour. I tol' one of 'em 'e knew a bloody sight more'n I did about the war" (*Privates*, p. 279).

It is not surprising then that so many participants' records of the war are apolitical attempts to explain the incomprehensible to themselves as well as to a world that never felt their ordeal along the pulses, to evoke the atmosphere which produced that ever present sense of worry that Ford Madox Ford wrote about in *No More Parades*, rather than to account for war origins. To get a sense of the proportion between those for whom the First World War was a personal experience and those for whom it was a politicizing experience, one needs to look at Robert Graves' account of Siegfried Sassoon's action of protest in *Goodbye to All That*. Sassoon's new state of consciousness is diagnosed as a case of battle fatigue. It would take still another half century before the gesture of Sassoon would be interpreted as an act of sanity.

Nine

Able Journalism,
Sob-Brotherly and Sane

To move from the individual perceptions of First World War
participants to a general historical overview of the opinions about
the origins of the war that were abroad in the late twenties and
thirties, we can expect to find a variety, many now modified by
the absence of war fever. A.J.P. Taylor summarizes that diversity
and points out how seriously held and widespread was the one
belief that the munitions makers were the prime movers:

> Few educated people now believed that the war had been
> caused by a deliberate German aggression, though one or two
> still held that Germany was more militaristic than others. In the
> general opinion, wars started by mistake – the view of Lord Grey;
> the negotiating machinery of the League would prevent these
> mistakes in the future. Or they were caused by great armaments,
> the view of Lloyd George; the remedy for this was disarmament.
> Or they were caused by "grievances"; the clear moral here was
> that these, now predominantly German, should be redressed. Or
> finally they were caused by "capitalism"; hence Labour's contribu-
> tion to peace was to bring capitalism to an end. A refinement of
> this last view was the doctrine, widely held in the thirties, that
> wars were deliberately fostered by the private manufacturers of
> armaments – a doctrine which produced a royal commission on
> the "war traffic" in this country in 1935 and a Senate inquiry in the
> United States.[1]

Looking back from 1949, a novelist whose introduction to the
world of strife was the Balkan war of 1912–1913 and who served in

the West African Frontier Force in the First World War, Joyce Cary, wrote: "People who said afterwards that it was the armament manufacturers ... who made the Kaiser war were of course writing history backwards, and history does not go backwards. The armaments manufacturers made war much less than the poets; and it is doubtful if wars need making, any more than the weather. There are always winds of opinion, clouds of imagination, changes of local and national temperature; and electricity is everywhere, lighting lamps and setting fire to steeples."[2] Despite the sanity of Joyce Cary's retrospective view, people did blame the munitions makers after the extent of their international dealings had come to the surface. As a consequence, their status as patriotic armorers of their own country diminished, and they were given the epithet "merchants of death," designating their involvement in the arming of all nations including enemies of their own.[3]

A writer who seized upon the anti-war sentiment of the country and enhanced it was Beverley Nichols, described by Robert Graves as an "able journalist of the 'sob-brother' variety" whose book, Cry Havoc! (1933) "...had a wide circulation, and was probably more effective in inculcating pacificism by its heart-to-heart unpolitical appeal than the carefully organized Left movements of the time."[4] In pointing out the book's weaknesses, an unsympathetic reviewer paradoxically revealed its strength as an instrument of popularization. Since the English and Americans are responsive to good journalism, wrote that reviewer, "...this book should have a large and responsive public and prove effective in raising the warmth of anti-war feeling several degrees.... The hackneyed horrors of war, past and future, are put through their paces like the bloodhounds in the old fashioned stock company presentation of 'Uncle Tom's Cabin.' Those who can gnash their teeth at Simon Legree or weep over East Lynne will be moved."[5]

Cry Havoc! is both an evocation of the atmosphere of impending war and an indictment of the munitions makers. It is fitting that the book opens with a long letter addressed "Dear H.G. Wells." Nichols, who calls himself "a pacifist of the pacifists," recalls a luncheon meeting at which he and Wells discussed the character of the next war. Nichols intended to declare himself a conscientious objector. Because of Wells, Nichols' "pacificism is no longer passivism." The inactive, plague-on-both-your-houses attitude of the ordinary pacifist may be noble but unrealistic because "...it ignores the fact that man is a social animal and is unable to stand aside on matters of national policy." Nichols began to write his book "...in the true anarchical peace-at-any-price spirit," prepared to wave the banner of peace throughout England and Europe.[6] But owing to the influence of H.G. Wells, he could not forget the realities of Europe in 1933. His reminder to himself of those realities supports Robert Graves' estimation of him as an able writer in his impassioned dedication to the cause of peace. The following passage also serves as an example of the evocative sweep of his writing:

> I am fighting in a world whose skies are slashed and tormented by the banners of discordant nationalities. I want to tear down those banners — the reds and the blues and the yellows — because they are shutting out the sun. I want to follow the white flag of peace only. But can I? In a world where Germany is a sullen, straining giant, rattling at the prison bars, where France, like a nervous gaoler, struts down the corridors of Europe, jangling her keys in her pocket, where the whole Italian population is being turned into an army drilled with operatic precision, and where the Russian limelight bathes both East and West in a strange glow that has never yet been seen on land or sea?
>
> Where does the white flag of peace lead a man through such lands? Can I keep it flying through Spain, for example, who has celebrated her entry into the revolutionary brotherhood of nations by plastering her coast with titanic guns? Or through Rumania, whose musical-comedy officers have their highly manicured hands tight around the nation's throat? Or through Greece and Turkey whose snarlings make a hell of the whole Near East? [*Cry Havoc!*, p. 7].

Young men in the early 1930's share Nichols' mood of helplessness and hopelessness in the face of the portents of war: "And there are thousands of young men in this country who, if they had the time would work out some similar confession of faith. For they feel, as I do, that life is not worth living under this shadow of war. The Spring is poisoned, the Summer is made a mockery, the Winter is a dark time of threatening winds and haunting dreads. All that is gay and lovely in life is tainted. How can a man think, let alone dream, when the hills and valleys are filled with the echo of soldiers marching?" (*Cry Havoc!*, pp. 19–20). Half the news of the week at the cinema shows armies on the march. Germany has got around her restriction to a 100,000 man army imposed by the Treaty of Versailles and could put a million men in the field in the first days of a war.

One of the now little remembered civilian war worries that Nichols plays upon in an attempt to alarm England to its vulnerability is the prospect of a gas attack from the air. We have forgotten the fascination that the thirties had for the untried possibilities of air power in war and the use of poison gas. London is wholly unprepared for that eventuality, despite the activities of an organization such as the Violet Cross which pushed for the universal use of gas masks. Moreover, it is impossible to outfit a whole city with gas masks or other suitable shelter for gas: "You cannot eat or drink or speak when you are wearing a gas-mask. You can do nothing but sit tight or lumber clumsily about. A minute proportion of the population might find refuge in shelters with filtered air – shelters which have yet to be built. The remainder would be defenseless" (*Cry Havoc!*, p. 61). And the use of gas by the enemy is a certainty, he warns emphatically: "But first we must make up our minds on one very important point, namely, that gas *will* be used.... Let nobody hope that this time it will be a 'gentleman's war...'" (*Cry Havoc!*, p. 62). Nor will he allow his readers the dubious reassurance of believing that the "damned" enemy will not get through, when the "damned English got through" on maneuvers: "In the most recent Defense of London Air Manoeuvres, out of a total of 250 aeroplanes which took part in a night attack on London, only *sixteen* were even discovered by searchlights, let alone shot down. And it must be remembered that even this meagre portion was arrived at when the defensive parties were on the alert and prepared for any emergency" (*Cry Havoc!*, p. 64). English, French, German and American experts all agree to the ease with which airplanes could drop on London gas which would envelop its population. Upon visiting his old school, Marlborough College, Nichols finds that its Officers' Training Program does not include gas or anti-aircraft training: "Anybody who fought in the Boer War would feel thoroughly at home in [the program's training manual]" (*Cry Havoc!*, p. 91).

This "pacifist of pacifists" sees himself as a Cassandra with a prophecy that must not go unheeded: "I should be the last person to claim that I have examined all the evidence. That would be the work of a lifetime, and no student of international affairs who is a preacher as well as a prophet can afford to give this study his life's endeavour, because he is so convinced of the urgency of the danger that he feels impelled to deliver his message before the flames have broken out" (*Cry Havoc!*, p. 118). *Si vis pacem, pare bellum* is the old lie. The next war will see untold casualties among the civilian population, and no system for defense can prevent it: "...another great war would almost certainly result in the extinction of tens of millions of Europe's civilian population by gas, by death from the air, by starvation or by disease. We have suggested (not without expert corroboration) that no amount of war 'preparation,' short of covering a whole country with a roof of steel, will be of any avail against the Furies that are straining at the leash. We have decided that such futile 'preparations' as we and other nations are making, are only likely to make it more difficult to hold that leash, are only likely to act as irritants ... that nothing will save civilization, if war breaks out" (*Cry Havoc!*, pp. 118–119).

If the political condition of Europe is in such a state of flux that today's prophecies become tomorrow's commonplaces, there remain abiding evils to attack. Behind all the worry about war is the armaments industry. Ending his letter to H.G. Wells, Nichols sounds very much like the Wells of 1914 when he asserts that the armaments industry is at the very center of the war *Geist* of the early 1930's. He refers to a pertinent report issued by the League of Nations in 1921, reciting the common accusations against the industry: that it created war scares, bribed officials, stimulated arms sales through false reports about military build-ups, and controlled the press. He proposes to make that abstract document come alive by taking the reader on a visit to an armaments firm.

Several English firms are put together to fashion the composite picture of "Armsville." The visitor learns that the industry is a competitive business under almost negligible governmental control and that it is flourishing in a time of widespread unemployment. Nichols is captivated by Armsville's wall charts of estimates which disclose that the firm was supplying fourteen nations simultaneously, two of whom were presently at war. A "bloody international" trade it is. Recalling the honors paid Sir Basil Zaharoff by the Empire when it made him a Doctor of Civil Laws (Oxford) and a Knight of the Grand Cross of the Bath, Nichols reflects on the irony that the gun salesman is honored in his own country while a pacifist is scorned. Undershaft's motto, "Unashamed," fits well with Armsville's, "We don't care who's having a whack at whom providing we get the order!" (Cry Havoc!, p. 29). Armsville stands for unfettered free enterprise in the tools of death: "More death, more dividends! More blood — more bonuses! ... Facts. That the government of this country, of every country, while raising its black-gloved hands in horror at the White Slave Traffic, at the Drug Traffic, at all other illegal traffics, yet gives its approval, its honour and blessing, to the traffic in death" (Cry Havoc!, pp. 31–32).

Finally, Nichols warns, peace is possible under capitalism only if no part of the system can get into a position to affect public policy. Here, he consults the experts and quotes Sir Arthur Salter as a representative of capitalism: "This danger exists in the case of the armaments business. The principal armament makers are concentrated in a few great companies: The Bethlehem Steel Company in America, Vickers Armstrong in England, Schneider-Creusot in France, Skoda in Czecho-Slovakia, and Mitsui in Japan. Their strength makes it possible for them to influence public opinion and political action very powerfully. Their financial interest is obviously that there shall be a general state of anxiety which increases the demand for munitions. I believe the only solution is that the private manufacture of arms should be prohibited."[7]

Among the considerable body of literature surrounding the munitions makers, there appeared in 1934 a book which seems to have been written as a repudiation of the emotionalism of the Nichols approach for a more dispassionate view of the subject. Despite its sensational title which had become by then something of a cliché, *Merchants of Death: A Study of the International Armament Industry* is remarkable for the restraint of its authors. The book adds to the discussion by disclosing some of the intricate international relationships of the industry, past and present; and it portentously evokes the spectacle of German rearmament.

A writer in the *Yale Review* commended the study for "...exposing the sinister record of the munitions makers in promoting sales by promoting wars," and found its balanced view a merit compared to that of another book on the subject reviewed with it.[8] In the Foreword to the *Merchants of Death*, Harry Elmer Barnes extols the authors for an unclouded presentation, the fruit of eschewing the rhetoric of the pacifist:

> Most accounts of the armament industry have been written by men and women who possess all the fervor of the valiant crusader against war. It is no disparagement of the usefulness and courage of the ardent pacifist to point out that this crusading psychology does not always supply the best background for a sane perspective on the causes of war. When a professional pacifist cuts loose on the armament industry, he frequently gives the impression that the armament makers constitute the chief menace to peace. By thus obscuring much more powerful factors which make for war, such writers render at least an indirect disservice to the cause of peace.[9]

Although the authors expose the corruption of the munitions industry with a thoroughness which would satisfy "the most determined pacifist," they also see the major flaw in the argument which assigns the blame for war to the machinations of the private armaments industry; namely, that the causes of war are not to be laid to any one group of human agents but to the whole of civilization: "Our civilization has permitted and even fostered war-making forces, such as nationalism, chauvinism, economic rivalry and competitive capitalism, imperialism and colonialism, political and territorial disputes, race hatred and pressure of population. The traditional way of establishing an equilibrium between these rival forces has been and is violence, armed warfare" (*Merchants*, p. 271). Thus the armaments industry is but a necessary adjunct to our present civilization: "A world which recognizes and expects war cannot get along without an enterprising, progressive, and up-to-date arms industry. All attempts to attack the problem of the arms maker in isolation — by nationalization or by international control — are almost certain to fail.... Wars are man-made, and peace, when it comes will also be man-made. Surely the challenge of war and of the armament maker is one that no intelligent or civilized being can evade" (*Merchants*, pp. 271–272).

"Patriotism is national; business is international," might well be added to Shaw's "Unashamed" as another motto of the munitions industry when one looks at examples of the absence of loyalty to its homeland. Engelbrecht and Hanighen recount instances of betrayal over the years. We are told that Hiram Maxim and Vickers Ltd. sold Maxim machine guns to the Boers with the probable knowledge that the British would be at war with them before long. With a sense of pride in his favorite invention, Maxim, the naturalized Englishman after whom Gissing's Lee Hannaford might easily have been patterned, records in his autobiography: "One [Maxim gun] manned by four Boers ... would put a whole battery of British artillery out of action in a very short time."[10] A well known account of international dealings that surfaced after the First World War was the dispute between Krupp and Vickers over royalties from shell fuses. During that war, Vickers was using artillery shell fuses patented by Krupp. Fallen behind their lines, German soldiers would find English shells with Krupp fuses in them. Krupp was to have received a royalty of one shilling per shell, and claimed a total of 123 million shillings. Being on the side of the loser, however, Krupp had to settle for less out of court (*Merchants*, p. 6).

Nor is following the "true faith of the Armourer" a thing of the past. We discover that two of Hitler's financial backers were directors of Czechoslovakia's Skoda Works which was under the control of the French Schneider-Creusot Company. Specific arms deals with Hitler are disclosed: an order for sixty British planes which the British government prevented from being filled; Schneider's sale in 1933 of four hundred tanks to Hitler routed through Holland. Perhaps the most complicated arrangement shows up in supplying of raw materials for explosives to Hitler's Germany:

> The Dura factory ... near Bordeaux, is shipping thousands of carloads of cellulose to Germany every year. This factory is mainly under British ownership.... The I.G. Farben Industrie in Germany which manufactures explosives from this cellulose is owned, to at least 75 per cent, by French capital. These facts are known in France but nothing is done about them, because the Dura factory is one of France's chief explosive factories in case of war, and because American manufacturers would immediately fill the German orders if the French did not. As for the French control of the German chemical industry, the government does not insist on the withdrawal of French capital for the simple reason that the British would immediately replace the French [*Merchants*, pp. 244–245].

The early 1930's offer little hope for peace. The First World War changed little in the way of political attitudes. The League of Nations and the Kellogg Pact have been ineffective in promoting the peaceful settlement of disputes among nations. Europe is rearming in 1933. Behind Hitler stands Thyssen, the steel baron of the Ruhr, who from 1930 to 1933 donated three million marks to the Nazi campaign chest. For his help Thyssen was given control of the German Steel Trust, the center of the armaments industry. Hitler's first budget of 800,000,000 marks is to be used chiefly for armaments. Iron imports rise each month:

Krupp is again producing cannon. The artillery range at Meppen is again alive with the testing of huge new guns. Armor plate of a new and special kind is also being made. The German chemical industry, always a world leader, is ready at a moment's notice, to produce deadly poisonous gases. Indications are that they are already being manufactured and stored for immediate use. Commercial airplanes, readily converted into military weapons, are at hand in great numbers. Subsidiary or friendly factories in Holland, Switzerland, Sweden, Italy, and Turkey are also ready to furnish arms without the least delay [*Merchants*, p. 244].

Ten

Agents, Assassins, and Armaments

Published in several languages between 1930 and 1933, the outpouring of books and articles on the munitions industry can be seen in the bibliography appended to *Merchants of Death*. For those three years Engelbrecht lists approximately forty items with such eye catching titles as *I Mercanti di Cannoni* (1932); "Munitions Morality" (1933); *The Bloody Traffic* (1933); *Salesmen of Death* (1933); "The Bloody International" (1931); *Les Marchands de Canons contra la Paix* (1932); "The Traffic in Death" (1932); *Patriotism, Ltd.* (1933); *Death and Profits* (1932); "Who Is Sir Basil Zaharoff?" (1932). Reviewers of *Merchants of Death* recommended it more for its sanity than its novelty. The writer in the *Yale Review* had stated that it belonged to a "now impressive body of literature." A reviewer in *TLS* referred to the book as "...this latest addition to a subject on which there is already so considerable a literature...." Philip Burnham remarked in *Commonweal*: "This book is certainly timely, and almost necessarily interesting, dealing as it does with the arms merchants and their romantic wares. However, the publicity recently given armaments manufacturers, if it has whetted the public appetite for the present volume, has also seriously cut down the novelty of the revelations. The whole exposé sounds, somehow, like a long preface."[1]

The public was exposed, then, to a plethora of information revealing that the munitions maker would willingly play the midwife to calamity at the expense not only of his fellow man but also his fellow countryman. Although judicious men put the blame for war is a larger context, recognizing that the problem was too

93

complex to be laid at the door of any single human agency, still the image of the armaments maker as fomentor of war appealed to popular sentiment. We might consider two reasons for the tenacity of the belief. First, there is the tendency of mankind when faced with complex insoluble problems to look for a single cause to explain the failings of a whole culture or civilization. That reaction, it might be added, is not confined to the ignorant. It is also to be found in more enlightened circles. Second, the dealer in the instruments of wholesale slaughter has an archetypal appeal. He is the evil principle: omnipotence in the service of indiscriminate destruction. The merchant of death exudes the odor of fire and brimstone, the charisma of the destroying angel.

With the public mind thus well stocked by exposés and revelations, we can turn to the literacy expression of that material in the 1930's. If for Philip Burnham *Merchants of Death* seemed "like a long preface" to the voluminous writings about the munitions makers, that considerable body of literature serves as a preface to some of Graham Greene's fiction. In three of his novels, Greene deals with the theme of internationalism in industry. He raises questions about the morality of the inner workings of international enterprise in *England Made Me* (1935); examines the relationship between neutrality and the supply of contraband in *The Confidential Agent* (1939); and capitalizes upon the contemporary publicity given the armaments industry in his use of the munitions maker as a promoter of war in *A Gun for Sale* (1936).

Munitions morality is not an issue in *England Made Me*, but we might do well to pause briefly over that book because it touches upon the problem of public trust in the international entrepreneur who, though first in peace in this novel, could very well be first in war. Behind the backdrop of railroad wheels and bus bodies in William Manchester's frontispiece of the late Alfred Krupp might be another depicting cannons and caissons. The scene is Stockholm. Erik Krogh is an industrialist, a capitalist, and "the richest man in Europe." Kate Farrant, his mistress, wants her brother Tony, sacked from his last job, to go to work for Krogh. Tony balks, saying he doesn't know Swedish. Kate tells him that he is "out of date," for "there are no foreigners in a business like Krogh's; we're internationalists there, we haven't a country. We aren't a little dusty City office which has been in the family for two hundred years."² Considering the possibility of employment with Krogh, Tony Farrant reminisces over his acquaintance with the name, revealing a sense of the omnipresence of Krogh and his products:

> Thinking of Krogh. "Use Krogh's. Krogh's are cheapest and best." That was ten years ago, no fifteen years ago, twenty years ago, shopping with the nurse at the general stores, stooping in the doorway under the baskets, brushing against the tins of weed-killer, examining the mowing machines, while my nurse bought Krogh's. Now they are not the cheapest and the best. They are the only. Krogh's in France, in Germany, in Italy, in Poland. Krogh's everywhere. "Buy Krogh's" has a different meaning now: ten per cent and rising daily.... Krogh like God Almighty in every home; impossible in the smallest cottage to do without Krogh; Krogh in England, in Europe, in Asia, but Krogh, like Almighty God, only a bloody man [*England Made Me*, pp. 22–23].

At this point, one might say that though there is something ominous about the size of the operation, there is also something benevolent. Krogh's appears no more fearsome than Sears and Roebuck of our time. The moral question that arises centers around how far the international entrepreneur will go to protect his many interests along with those of his shareholders and employees. At a crucial juncture, Krogh's survival on the Stock Exchange depends upon maintaining the appearance of soundness for just one week at which time an American subsidiary company will be launched and the whole Krogh empire will be saved. Krogh's reaction is a little fraud on the Exchange and the frame-up of the leader of a strike which threatens the delicate juggling of shares. Add to that the murder of Tony Farrant who talked too freely to the Press and who decided not to stay a week in Stockholm until the American subsidiary got started, after which what he said would not have mattered.

Greene classifies *England Made Me* as one of his novels, not as one of his "entertainments." As such, the presence of deceit and violence is less liable to be construed as the staple ingredients of the thriller. The novel is a thoughtful consideration of how far, in the midst of the economic insecurity of the mid 1930's, the industrialist whose shares are on all the Exchanges of the world is willing to go to preserve the trust that the public, who hangs on his every word and watches his every physical movement, has for the name of Krogh. That fraud, battery, and murder are Krogh's response makes the image of the international producer of "the cheapest and the best" of peacetime goods not much more attractive than that of the international armorer.

More within the scope of this study is *The Confidential Agent*, a novel in which the industrialist appears as the war profiteer who, though a neutral, will sell his coal legally or illegally to the side in a civil war which offers him the greatest profit. Designated by Greene as one of his entertainments, the novel is above the cut of the ordinary thriller even by the conventions of that genre. The political idealism and the humanity of Agent D., not untouched by a realistic appraisal of the behavior of both sides in a civil war, imbue the book with the spirit of hope for a better world to come after the fighting is over. The grave and inexperienced D. undertakes his mission in the foreign land of England faced at every step with the practical question, "Whom can you trust?"

Before the civil war began in his country, Spain presumably, D. was an academic, a professor of Romance languages whose reputation was made by his discovery of a suppressed version of the Song of Roland establishing the real hero as Oliver and exposing Roland as a warrior who sacrificed his men to his own greater glory. But both D.'s occupation and the glorious chivalry of war have changed. Modern war materials are not as romantic as they were in the Middle Ages. Modern warfare depends as much on such prosaic raw materials as coal as upon weapons. D. explains to Rose Cullen, the coal owner's daughter: "Wars to-day are not what they were in Roland's time. Coal can be more important than tanks. We've got more tanks than we want.... The coal is as good as a whole fleet of the latest bombers."[3]

In the course of the war, D. has been sent to England by the recognized government of his country to buy the coal that will enable his side to conduct the war indefinitely. Owing to the general depression in trade, the collieries of Lord Benditch have been closed for some time. The transaction would be profitable to both. The rebel government has sent over Agent L. to buy the same coal. From the moment of his disembarkation in England, D. has had to ward off repeated attempts by L.'s henchmen to steal his credentials without which he cannot do business with the English coal owners, without which he cannot be trusted.

The theme of trust is central to the novel. Where it touches upon the coal owners most directly is in the statement by Rose Cullen, Lord Benditch's daughter but a sympathizer of D.'s, that no one can be trusted in all things. Her father believes in the virtue of trust but where business is involved, the cash nexus and iron clad contract prevails: "...there's no trust anywhere. I'd never seen a face that looked medium honest. I mean about everything. My father's people—they're honest about—well, food and love per-haps—they have stuffy contented wives, anyway—but where coal is concerned—or the workmen.... If you hope for anything at all from them, for God's sake don't breathe melodrama—or sentiment. Show them a cheque-book, a contract—let it be a cast iron one" (*Agent*, p. 81). Among Lord Benditch's partners only Forbes can be relied upon about coal, Rose explains to D.; but like everyone else he is not honest about everything: "You can trust Forbes ... about coal, I mean. Not of course all around the clock. He's dishonest about his name—he was a Jew called Furtstein. And he's dishonest in love. He wants to marry me. That's how I know. He keeps a mistress in Shepherd's Market" (*Agent*, p. 82).

After several mishaps, D. meets the coal owners over a table: "It was like the final viva voce examination for a degree" (*Agent*, p. 115). There is an air of unreality about the meeting. One of the coal owners is asleep behind a couch; another sits at the table drawing pictures of girls with "goo-goo eyes." It hardly seemed the place wherein the fate of the agent's government should be decided. The mine owners want to be paid a full market price in gold and a thirty-five percent profiteer's bonus upon delivery. One of them, Brigstock, tells D.: "We are business men: we are not politicians or crusaders." Lord Benditch enlarges upon Brigstock's statement by saying that he and his partners might get a better offer, meaning from L., the agent of the rebels, who has been trying to thwart D. all along. Shunning melodrama, D. shows an unexpected turn at bargaining. He reminds Lord Benditch of the future. If the rebels win, they may no longer be customers, for they have other allies. Benditch replies that business men take short views: "That is looking very far ahead. What concerns us is immediate profit." D., however, wins them over by pointing out that the rebels' position is not legitimate: "You may find their gold is less certain than our paper. After all, it's stolen. We should bring an action.... And there's your government. To send coal to the rebels might prove illegal" (*Agent*, p. 118). A bargain is struck, but D. discovers that his pocket has been picked just before the meeting. With his credentials gone, there can be no contract. He tries to explain that his credentials were stolen but the mine owners are unmoved: "It was like the putting up of shutters at night to guard—well, the Royal mistresses and the Etty. Benditch, Fetting, Brigstock—they all became expressionless as if he had told a dirty story in unsuitable company" (*Agent*, p. 122).

Agent L. carries the day and signs a contract on behalf of the rebel government. D. does not think the coal can get out of the ports because of the neutrality agreement. But since it was against English law to trade with the rebels, L. had arranged that the coal go by way of Holland. All that there is left for D. to do is make the desperately idealistic effort of going up to the mining towns and addressing the miners, telling them about the illegality of the transaction and about the final destination of the coal. Rose Cullen advises him that his move will not work. The miners have been unemployed too long and altruism may be beyond them: "You

don't know how things are here. You've never seen a mining village
when all the pits are closed. You've lived in a revolution — you've
had too much cheering and shouting and waving of flags.... I've
been with my father to one of these places. He was making a tour —
with royalty. There's no spirit left" (*Agent*, p. 196). On his way to
the Benditch mines, D. sees evidence of an industry that has not
seen slack times: a munitions train at a station headed not for the
mines but for some unknown destination.

Benditch's agent appears in the mining town to announce the
opening of the pits. D. knows it will be difficult to convince these
people to support him by not going to work: "He was reminded of
an occasion when in the hungry capital a rumour spread that food
had arrived: he had watched them swarming down on to the quay,
just like this. It hadn't been food but tanks, and they watched the
tanks unloaded with angry indifference. Yet they had needed the
tanks" (*Agent*, p. 228). The miners "...were the people he was
fighting for — and he had a frightening sense now that they were his
enemies: he was there to stand between them and hope" (*Agent*,
p. 229). D. discovers that some miners, like their employers, are
indifferent to where the strategic material goes. When he tells a
miner's wife that the men should refuse to mine the coal, she is
dumbfounded: "You're off your nut.... You're crazy.... Why should
we care?" (*Agent*, p. 230). Telling them that their depression is
over, the coal owner's man assures the miners that they shall be
working every day for a year. D. reminds Bates, the union leader,
and the crowd, who are under the impression that the coal is going
to Holland only, that the unions said that they would never work
for the rebel government: "I know this means a lot to you. But
it means everything to us.... Why do they want *your* coal? Because the miners at home won't work for them. They shoot them,
but they won't work..." (*Agent*, pp. 234–235). Joe Bates is inclined
toward the procedural in this case: "I think the best thing we can
do ... is to ask a definite assurance from Lord Benditch's agent that
the coal is going to Holland — and only Holland" (*Agent*, p. 235).
Benditch's man is only too ready to lie by affirming that is so.

All is up. D. has failed to persuade the miners not to work. Moreover, the police are after him for sundry charges. A gang of youthful *dei ex machina* come out of nowhere to hide him. They heard his speech to the miners and despite the fact that their fathers work in the mines, the boys want to stop the pits from working. It is not a political act, theirs. They merely want to bid defiance to their elders. On condition that he give them his gun, the boys promise to get dynamite and blow up the pits. "Why? ... Fun" (*Agent*, p. 241). The boys manage to blow up the explosives shed but no pits. D. thinks his last chance is gone, but the publicity of the explosion made up for the failure of persuasion. Later, Forbes, who for Rose's sake helps D. to get out of the country, tells him that the rebel coal deal is off. Coal owners cannot conduct illegal business in the light of publicity.

> "But that explosion at Benditch—you know, it blew L.'s contract sky-high.... You haven't got the coal yourself but L. hasn't got it either. We had a meeting early this morning. We've cancelled the contract. The risk is too great."
> "The risk?"
> "To reopen the pits and then find the Government stepping in. You couldn't have advertised the affair better if you'd bought the front page of the *Mail*. Already there's been a leading article— about political gangsters and the civil war being fought on English soil. We had to decide whether to sue the paper for libel or cancel the contract and announce that we had signed in good faith under the idea the coal was going to Holland. So we cancelled" [*Agent*, pp. 267–268].

As a political document *The Confidential Agent* demonstrates that the pursuit of profit acknowledges no national boundaries, recognizes the justice or injustice of no cause. And the industrialist is not the only one without honor. Every man has his price. The cabinet ministers of D.'s government, and his fellow agents as well, will also sell out for a better deal. But the novel rises above the topicalities of the thirties, momentous as they are—the Spanish Civil War and the international interests of dealers in strategic materials—and treats philosophically as well as practically the question of the nature of trust. Every man has his price, but every man can be trusted in some things. On the other hand, those who are capable of complete trust are vulnerable. Those like D.'s young chambermaid, innocent in her wholehearted loyalty to D., nourished by the romantic fiction she has read, perish; just as did Roland's warriors who blindly trusted their lord to the end when, according to D., Oliver, the true hero of Roncesvalles, saw that Roland was betraying them in his concern for personal glory.

Despite the gravity of D.'s mission, the book is not without its lighter side. The amateur agent and former academic has a penchant for the melodramatic because he is uncertain about how an agent should behave. And the atmosphere of international intrigue is counterpointed with comic irony by the naïveté of the Entrenationo Language Center whose supporters believe in the efficacy of an international language as a means to international understanding.

The Confidential Agent enjoyed a wide popularity particularly after having been put on the screen. *A Gun for Sale* also reached a large public when it was made into an American film a few years after its publication in 1936, bearing the Americanized title of "This Gun for Hire." Publishing this novel the year after the inquiry of a royal commission into the armaments industry, Greene out-Herods Herod by portraying a munitions magnate who almost sets off the next world war because business is slack. That deed surpasses anything that the critics of the private armaments firms could come up with in the way of evidence against the merchant of death in the flesh. Sir Basil Zaharoff might sell his beloved Greece one submarine and then persuade her (and his) natural enemy Turkey that if Greece has one, Turkey should have two submarines. But such a feat of actuality pales in comparison with that of Greene's Sir Marcus, head of Midland Steel. Greene puts into fiction the fantasy of the single-cause-for-war mentality, a literal enactment of the belief that munitions makers were war promoters. Sir Marcus arranges the assassination of a Czech minister with the blame cast where it was in the First World War—on Serbia.

Put by Greene in the same category of "an entertainment" as
The Confidential Agent, A Gun for Sale is not a throw-away
thriller. Greene shows an interest in matters of form as well as
theme. There is a persistent use of dramatic irony, at times heavy-
handed and at times subtle. The fantastic plot takes up the issues
of munitions morality, but if the plot is fantastic, the thirties' fear
of an impending war that permeates the air is very real. A war is
coming, one senses, with or without the machinations of the munitions maker.

The possibilities for dramatic irony are offered from the start
following the assassination of the old Czech Socialist minister.
After Raven kills the old man, he comes back to England to be
paid. England's press is filled with news of an ultimatum and
Europe mobilizing. After all, we are told, the last war began with a
murder even if that one was an archduke's and this an old politician's. Not trusted by his employers, Raven is paid off in stolen
notes by Cholmondeley-Davis acting for Sir Marcus. Very quickly
the police are after Raven on the charge of having passed the stolen
notes. At a newspaper office ironic parallels are drawn between
Raven the suspected thief and the still unknown assassin. Unaware
of the connection, the reporters talk about the two news stories
at once:

> "He got clean away with a policeman watching the front door.
> The Flying Squad's out. He's armed. The police are taking re-
> volvers. It's a lovely story."
> "...Armed! Go away and put your head in a glass of milk. We'll
> all be armed in a day or two.... It's clear as daylight a Serb shot
> him. Italy's supporting the ultimatum. They've got forty-eight
> hours to climb down. If you want to buy armaments shares,
> hurry and make your fortune."[4]

The prospect of a gas attack that Beverley Nichols made so
much of in *Cry Havoc!* is skillfully employed by Greene throughout the book. One reporter promises to write an article on the need
of gas masks and gas practice for all, thus foreshadowing the last

scenes in the book – the gas practice which enables Raven to get to Sir Marcus disguised by a gas mask. Greene makes use of dramatic irony in another scene by drawing a parallel between Raven and his assassin's act. We are not permitted to forget about gas or munitions shares. Hunted for the stolen notes, Raven goes to a sleazy abortionist for an operation on the hare-lip which so readily identifies him. The doctor brings out gas instead of an anaesthetic. Once more Greene moves from the particular case of Raven to the general world crisis he has caused by his act and behind it all, the suggestion of the munitions mentality of Sir Marcus. War, gas masks, munitions – the concerns of the novel and the fears of the age in a nutshell:

> "Stop," Raven said, "You're not going to give me gas."
> "It would hurt without it, old man," Dr. Yogel said, approaching with the mask, "it would hurt like hell."
> Raven sat up and pushed the mask aside. "I won't have it ... not gas. I've never had gas. I've never passed out yet. I like to see what's going on."
> Dr. Yogel laughed gently and pulled at Raven's lip in a playful way. "Better get used to it, old man. We'll all be gassed in a day or two."
> "What do you mean?"
> "Well, it looks like war, doesn't it?" Dr. Yogel said, talking rapidly and unwinding more tube, turning screws in a soft, shaking, inexorable way. "The Serbs can't shoot a Minister of War like that and get away with it. Italy's ready to come in. And the French are warming up. We'll be in it ourselves inside a week."
> Raven said: "All that because an old man...." He explained: "I haven't read the papers."
> "I wish I had known beforehand," Dr. Yogel said, making conversation, fixing his cylinder. "I'd have made a fortune in munitions shares. They've gone up to the sky, old man" [*Gun*, p. 32].

Greene's use of dramatic irony is somewhat ponderous but where irony emerges from ambiguity the effects are more subtle. The ambiguity of the title, for example, is completely lost in the American screen title, "This Gun for Hire," because the focus is

then wholly upon Raven as hired killer. The ambiguity of "A Gun
for Sale," on the other hand, gives proportionate emphasis upon
both Raven and Sir Marcus. It is a shingle both can hang out. The
paid killer's act will put the merchant of death back into business.
Ambiguity adeptly contrived emanates from Greene's device of re-
cording conversations on more than one subject going on simultaneously with the antecedents of pronouns left indefinite. Out in
the street, Raven overheads a conversation about the impending
war and a literary discussion about Galsworthy shuffled together.
The tribute to Galworthy's humanity applies also to the assassinated minister of war after we learn about his slum clearing project
paid for with money from his country's defense budget:

> "That's why I always liked Galsworthy. He was a gentleman.
> You knew where you were, if you know what I mean."
> "It always seemed to be the Balkans."
> "I liked *Loyalties*."
> "He was such a humane man."
>
> "They say the fleet...."
> "He makes you *think*. That's what I like."
>
> "Anything in the papers?"
> "Nothing new."
>
> "He used to subscribe heavily to the Anti-Vivisection Society.
> Mrs. Milbanke told me. She showed me one of his cheques with
> his signature."
> "He was really humane."
> "And a *really* great writer" [*Gun*, pp. 36–37].

Writing in the wake of publicity about munitions makers,
Greene's challenge as a writer of "an entertainment" was to fulfill
the fantasy of a reading public. In that world of fantasy, what
would a merchant of death look like? Act like? To answer that
question with reference to the real world would be to miss an op-
portunity. To say that the munitions maker looked not very

different from an oil company executive, though that is true, would
be to deny the world of the imagination and take up the pen of the
social historian. If the merchant of death was a moral dwarf in the
popular esteem, then the novelist was not fulfilling his readers'
expectations by presenting him as an ordinary businessman. The
public did not want to look at Dorian Gray; they wanted to see his
picture behind the curtain, not the morally inscrutable Dorian but
the portrait with all the signs of moral corruption on a grand scale
visibly evident.

John Ruskin once called Dickens' Josiah Bounderby of Coke-
town a "dramatic monster" and regretted that by overdoing that
character Dickens obscured the truth of his case against industrialism. By comparison, Graham Greene's Sir Marcus, head of Midland Steel, might be called an "expository monster," but Greene is
not really trying to make a case against the evils of industrialism.
Although he sets off the action by hiring Raven to kill the Czech
minister, Sir Marcus is otherwise a static figure. Whatever else we
learn about him comes more from Greene's exposition than from
Sir Marcus' dramatic action.

Upon our first acquaintance with Sir Marcus, he is trying to
arrange another murder, this time, a legal murder. Having heard
that Raven has evaded the police and is somewhere in Nottwich,
the home of Midland Steel, the armaments magnate wants Chief
Constable Calkin to instruct his men to shoot to kill Raven since
he has now served his purpose and might cause trouble. In de-
lineating a thoroughly diabolical character, only the most single-
minded novelist with a cause will not concede something to that
character's profession, class or country if only to avoid the accusation of stereotyping. Harriet Beecher Stowe conceded such a point
to the South when she made Simon Legree a Yankee. Graham
Greene accords to Englishborn industrialists their humanity and
love of country by making Sir Marcus a foreigner, a cosmopolite,
perhaps a Jew: "He spoke with the faintest foreign accent and it was
difficult to determine whether he was Jewish or of an ancient English family. He gave the impression that very many cities had

rubbed him smooth. If there was a touch of Jerusalem, there was also a touch of St. James, if of Vienna or some Central European ghetto, there were also marks of the most exclusive clubs of Cannes" (*Gun*, p. 137).

Like Sir Basil Zaharoff, Sir Marcus was one of the very rich and a mystery man of Europe. No one knew the whole story of his life. In this respect, too, a fitting descriptive tag applicable to him is that of "no-nation Midas," a designation given by C.E. Montague in his novel *Rough Justice* (1926) to the financial adventurers who made money out of South Africa at the turn of the century:

> Everyone knew a lot about Sir Marcus. The trouble was, what they knew was contradictory. There were people who, because of his Christian name, believed that he was a Greek; others were quite as certain he was born in a ghetto. His business associates said that he was of an old English family; his nose was no evidence either way; you found plenty of noses like that in Cornwall and the west country. His name did not appear in *Who's Who*, and an enterprising journalist who once tried to write his life found extraordinary gaps in registers; it wasn't possible to follow any rumour to its source. There was even a gap in the legal records of Marseilles where one rumour said that Sir Marcus as a youth had been charged with theft from a visitor to a bawdy house. Now he sat there in the heavy Edwardian dining room brushing biscuit crumbs from his waistcoat, one of the richest men in Europe [*Gun*, pp. 139–140].

In addition to the uncertainty of his origins and his questionable national loyalties, Sir Marcus is presented as physically unattractive by virtue of his extreme age. He is avarice grown to decrepitude and left with little more than an instinct for preservation of self and fortune: "He was a very old, sick man with a little wisp of white beard on his chin resembling chicken fluff. He gave the effect of having withered inside his clothes like a kernel on a nut..." (*Gun*, p. 137). "He was a man almost without pleasures; his most vivid emotion was venom, his main object defense: defense of his fortune, of the pale flicker of vitality he gained each year in the Cannes sun, of his life. He was quite content to eat cheese biscuits to the end of them if eating biscuits would extend his days" (*Gun*, p. 139). When Raven confronts the old man with his gun telling him that he would not have assassinated the old Minister had he known he was a friend of the poor, Sir Marcus is unaffected; he is mummified, physically beyond fear, psychologically beyond cowardice: " 'That was your doing. How do you like that?' But the old man sat there apparently unmoved: old age had killed the imagination. The deaths he ordered were no more real to him than the deaths he read about in the newspapers. A little greed (for his milk), a little vice (occasionally to put his old hand inside a girl's blouse and feel the warmth of life), a little avarice and calculation (half a million against a death), a very small persistent, almost mechanical, sense of self-preservation, these were his only passions" (*Gun*, pp. 215-216).[5]

If some dimensions of Sir Marcus are unfathomable, his motives for arranging the assassination are uncomplicatedly economic. Midland Steel once employed fifty thousand men but not long ago had to cut down even on the number of their doorkeepers. When the frightened Cholmondeley-Davis is cornered by Raven, he confesses that the murder was Sir Marcus' idea: "We were on our last legs here. We'd got to make money. It was worth more than a half million to him" (*Gun*, p. 215). With four countries at war, "...the consumption of munitions [would] have risen to a million pounds a day" (*Gun*, p. 149). Sir Marcus had many international friends and if one could not export arms directly, still there was money to be made exporting raw materials that were as essential to a war effort as weapons. There is a suggestion here too that the Government would close its eyes to the final destination of strategic materials. Sir Marcus reads his ticker tape and is pleased to find that shares in Midland Steel are doing better than they had since Armistice Day:

> Armaments shares continued to rise, and with them steel. It made no difference at all that the British government had stopped

all export licenses; the country itself was now absorbing more armaments than it had ever done since the peak year of Haig's assault on the Hindenburg Line. Sir Marcus had many friends, in many countries; he wintered with them regularly at Cannes or in Soppelsa's yacht off Rhodes; he was the intimate friend of Mrs. Cranbeim. It was impossible now to export arms, but it was still possible to export nickel and most of the other metals which were necessary to the arming of nations. Even when war was declared, Mrs. Cranbeim was able to say quite definitely that ... the British Government would not forbid the export of nickel to Switzerland or other neutral countries so long as the British requirements were first met. So the future really was very rosy indeed, for you could trust Mrs. Cranbeim's word. She spoke directly from the horse's mouth, if you could so describe the elder statesman whose confidence she shared" [*Gun*, pp. 148-149].

If Sir Marcus is an imaginative recreation of the thirties' pre-occupation with the activities of the merchant of death, Anne Crowder is the carrier of the burden of that decade's fear of war. At one point Anne says "Men were fighting beasts, they needed war." Sir Marcus arranges an assassination for Raven to carry out. Detective Mather pursues Raven as a suspected thief. A news reporter and an abortionist go about their work making jokes about buying armaments shares. Constable Calkin dreams of "giving hell to the Conchies" as he did in the last war. All of which is to say that men lack the imagination of disaster; they can hear the bad news of the world but it does not penetrate. They are bent upon the details of the immediate task at hand. It is the feminine sensibility that pauses to reflect over the meaning of "ultimatum" and "Europe mobilising" to humanity.

On her way to a provincial touring company, Anne wonders whether the war will break out before she sees her friend Mather again. At Nottwich, home of Midland Steel, Anne meets Raven looking for Cholmondeley-Davis who, she discovers, is a backer of her theatrical production. She knows that the threat of war might be averted if Raven finds Cholmondeley-Davis and his employer

Sir Marcus, but she decides to remain neutral, neither to help Raven nor to give him away, until she walks out of the theatre into the street and sees in the faces of the crowd the mute apprehension of war, so unlike the delirium which hysterically welcomed the First World War:

> But what she saw there made her pause. The street was full of people; they stretched along the southern pavement past the theatre entrance, as far as the market. They were watching the electric bulbs above Wallace's, the big drapers, spelling out the night's news. She had seen nothing like it since the last election, but this was different, because there were no cheers. They were reading of the troop movements over Europe, of the precautions against gas raids. Anne was not old enough to remember how the last war began; but she had read of the crowds outside the Palace, the enthusiasm, the queues at the recruiting offices, and that is how she had pictured every war beginning. She had feared it only for herself and Mather. She had thought of it as a personal tragedy played out against a background of cheers and flags. But this was different: this silent crowd wasn't jubilant, it was afraid. The white faces were turned towards the sky with a kind of secular entreaty; they weren't praying to any God; they were just willing that the electric bulbs would tell a different story. They were caught there on the way back from work, with tools and attache cases, by the rows of bulbs, spelling out complications they simply didn't understand [*Gun*, pp. 66–67].

Touched by the almost bovine entreaty of those faces, Anne decides to help Raven find Cholmondeley and Sir Marcus before the police find Raven. But Cholmondeley finds her first. Bound, gagged, and propped up inside the chimney of a fireplace, she meditates over the prospect of war, particularly the defenselessness of infants. Rescued by Raven, her resolve to prevent the war is stronger still: "I thought a lot about that war. I read somewhere, but I'd forgotten, about how babies can't wear gas masks because there's not enough air for them.... There wasn't much air there. It made things sort of vivid. I thought, we've got to stop it. It seems silly, doesn't it, us two, but there's nobody else" (*Gun*, p. 127).

In the physical universe of *A Gun for Sale*, Anne's move to prevent war is the equal and opposite reaction to Sir Marcus' action. She puts out the fire. The fact that in this case the arsonist is apprehended is a bonus. On the level of plot, then, there is a balance of opposites between those who try to start a war and those who stop it. Necessary as it was, Anne's move was a reflex whose purpose was to help forward the plot. But what about the moral universe of the novel? In the figure of Sir Marcus, Greene has introduced a morally unscrupulous foreign element into the England of his story. How is a moral balance achieved? How are we assured that Sir Marcus is an anomaly and reassured that his act is alien to the English grain, that England is vital, healthy and ever ready to disavow the undesirable who is not her kind? Chief Constable Calkin, bumbling and self-important though he be, and the scrupulosity of English police procedure affirm that Sir Marcus' way is not the English way.

When we first meet the chief constable of Nottwich, we find a smug provincial who does not look upon the likelihood of war with great aversion. He is reminiscing with great satisfaction over his experience on the home front in the last war: "The chief constable was fat and excited. He had made a lot of money as a tradesman and during the war had been given a commission and the job of presiding over the local military tribunal. He prided himself on having been a terror to pacifists" (*Gun*, p. 84). Calkin recalls the exaltation of possessing the rank of major at that time: "Major Calkin, he thought wistfully, Major Calkin. The trouble is I'm a man's man. Looking out of the window of his dressing-room at the spread lights of Nottwich he remembered the war, the tribunal, the fun it had all been giving hell to the conchies. His uniform still hung there..." (*Gun*, p. 134).

But with Sir Marcus a local power in Nottwich, a commission is not to be had without a *quid pro quo*. Telling him that Raven is dangerous, Sir Marcus wants Calkin and his men to shoot Raven on sight. The head of Midland Steel tries to bribe the chief constable by dangling in front of him a colonelcy at a local training depot for the oncoming war. When Calkin hesitates, Sir Marcus threatens him with the loss of his present position as constable. Comfort loving Calkin may be, but to him to shoot on sight is murder. Moreover, he does not think the men under him would obey such an order. As much as the comic constable wants both his present job and a colonelcy in the immediate future, what Sir Marcus has advanced is unthinkable. All he needed to do to agree to the proposition is to telephone Sir Marcus, "But he sat there doing nothing, a small plump bullying hen-pecked profiteer" (*Gun*, p. 147). Though a comic figure, Calkin and the English restrictions on police violence are a reassurance that constitutional English decency and fair play will not be overpowered by the impulse to self-aggrandisement or the pressure of "foreign" elements like Sir Marcus. We are left with the feeling that this is England, and those things that one reads about occurring in foreign countries just do not happen here:

> "He wanted me to give orders to your men to shoot this fellow on sight. I told him I couldn't. Now I can't help thinking we might have saved two lives."
> "Don't you worry, sir," the superintendent said, "we couldn't have taken orders like that. Not from the Home Secretary himself."
> "He was an odd fellow," Major Calkin said. "He seemed to think I'd be certain to have a hold over some of you. He promised me all kinds of things" [*Gun*, p. 230].

Having seen the fatal results of the shootout with Raven, the chief constable is sickened by violence and not so certain that he wants to preside over the military tribunal for conscientious objectors in the next war.

As in *The Confidential Agent*, Greene moves away from the concerns of the age when he takes up the theme of trust, this time in the solitary figure of Raven. Son of an executed murderer and a suicide, he has always been alone. Even his own kind betray him. Cholmondeley double-crosses him, and Dr. Yogel wants to turn him in for a reward. He begins to trust Anne but she must inevitably tell Mather that Raven, not a Serb, killed the Minister so that the Czechs can be placated. As he learns to trust Anne, he develops a glimmer of a social conscience. At first he does not understand or care about the war. In his ignorance he feels a strange pride in having started all this talk about ultimatums and mobilization. Seeking only personal revenge, he goes after Sir Marcus; but after meeting Anne and discovering that the man he killed was a poor man who cleared slums, the confluence of feelings of personal revenge and the stirrings of a sense of social injustice which he unwittingly abetted by his act rushes him along to a reckoning in the munition maker's room.

Anne prevents a war, but readers of fiction in 1936 know that the war is merely postponed: "This darkening land, flowing backwards down the line, was safe for a few more years. [Mather] was a countryman, and he didn't ask for more than a few years' safety at a time for something he so dearly loved. The precariousness of its safety made it only the more precious" (*Gun*, p. 242).

Bombers and poison gas, two instruments of *Schrecklichkeit* in the modern arsenal, are never far from the consciousness of George Bowling in George Orwell's *Coming Up for Air* (1939). With a windfall of seventeen quid in his pocket, Bowling takes a train to Lower Binfield to look for the civilization that existed there before the First World War when he was a child. As an English bomber flies over the train, one of the passengers glances at it; and all share his thoughts: "In two years' time, one year's time, what shall we be doing when we see one of those things? Making a dive for the cellar and wetting our bags with fright."[6]

Bowling speculates upon where the bombs will fall. The newspapers are falsely optimistic with their reassurances that the country can be protected from enemy bombing planes. One journalist goes so far as to say that bombers will not do much damage because improvements in English anti-aircraft gunnery will force enemy aircraft to fly at too high an altitude to permit accuracy. All that means to Bowling is that the bombs will miss military installations and explode on streets of lower middle class homes much like his own. London is a prime target for enemy bomber crews, the more so because of the barbarism of twentieth century warfare which recognizes no distinction between soldiers and civilians and whose *Realpolitik* makes a virtue of the surprise attack. Since London is composed of twenty miles of houses in any direction, enemy bombardiers can unload their deadly cargoes without even aiming. Hitler will probably not declare war beforehand, but will send his airborne terror over England during a peace conference. It will happen on a quiet morning when office clerks are walking to work across London Bridge, when housewives are hanging out their laundry, and when pet birds are singing. The bombs will fall; the clothes will be bloodied; and the songbirds will sing over the dead.

Arriving at Lower Binfield, Bowling sees a group of fifty children marching in military fashion while going through an air raid practice. They are carrying signs announcing their preparedness. When he asks why the children are drilling, Bowling is told that it is a process of conditioning for the inevitable. The children are taught that bombs are certain to fall on English towns so that they will unquestioningly make a dive for the nearest air raid shelter when the time comes. The test comes very soon. Two English bombers fly over one end of the town. One of them accidentally drops a bomb. It explodes and everyone thinks that the Germans have attacked without warning. When no additional bombs fall, Bowling gets off the pavement and sees what resembles a gathering of the Velvet Cross organization—fifty children wearing gas masks of the snout design. Owing to his dazed condition, the group looks momentarily to Bowling like a herd of pigs, a sea of pig faces. Shaking off his fit of association, Bowling realizes that he is observing school children in gas masks making for a bomb shelter.

After viewing the bomb damage, Bowling bids farewell to Lower Binfield. He had gone there in search of a past that did not exist, and the accidental bombing which presages the future underscores the nonexistence of the dream of his boyhood before the First World War. In one way, Bowling's vision of the future magnifies the question William Morris raised about a lesser war: "...and if we are overpowered—what then?" H.G. Wells' opinion of a German victory in the First World War foreshadows the emotional reaction of a later generation to the prospect of defeat by Hitler's thousand year Reich: "The fate of the world under triumphant Prussianism and Kruppism for the next two hundred years is not worth discussing." That later generation reading its newspapers and listening to its radios felt the full force of that dread of defeat. But in another way, Bowling envisions a change not as simply defined as the victory of one political entity or one economic ideology over another but the totalitarianization of an entire civilization, the end result of which, it might be added, would make the munitions maker, capitalism, and even war as we know it irrelevant:

> War is coming. 1941, they say. And there'll be plenty of broken crockery, and little houses ripped open like packing-cases, and the guts of the chartered accountant's clerk plastered over the piano that he's buying on the never-never. But what does that kind of thing matter anyway? I'll tell you what my stay in Lower Binfield had taught me, and it was this. *It's all going to happen.* All the things you've got in the back of your mind, the things you're terrified of, the things that you tell yourself are just a nightmare or only happen in foreign countries. The bombs, the food queues, the rubber truncheons, the barbed wire, the coloured shirts, the slogans, the enormous faces, the machine-guns squirting out of bedroom windows. It's all going to happen. I know it—at any rate, I knew it then. There's no escape. Fight against it if you like, or look the other way and pretend not to notice, or grab your spanner and rush out to do a bit of face-smashing along with the others. But there's no way out. It's just something that's got to happen.... What's coming afterwards I don't know, it hardly even interests me. I only know that if there's anything you care a curse about, better say good-bye to it now, because everything you've ever known is going down, down, into the muck, with the machine guns rattling all the time [*Air*, pp. 267, 269].

Chapter Notes

Chapter One

1. L. Woodward, *The Age of Reform, 1815–1870*, 2nd ed. (Oxford: Clarendon Press, 1962), pp. 120–122; Elie Halévy, *The Age of Peel and Cobden: A History of the English People, 1841–1852* (London: Benn, 1947), pp. 127–129.

2. His reputation as an "International Man" rests upon his policy of non-intervention, at root a peace policy. J.A. Hobson, *Richard Cobden: The International Man* (New York: Holt, 1919), pp. 387–409.

3. *The Three Panics* [1862] in *The Political Writings of Richard Cobden*, ed. Sir Louis Mallet (London: Ridgeway, 1878), p. 390. During the second "panic" in 1852, the "Invasionists" influenced Parliament to pass a Militia Bill. John Bright fought the measure but lost. Herman Ausubel, *John Bright, Victorian Reformer* (New York: John Wiley, 1966), p. 53.

4. Cobden, *Three Panics, Political Writings*, p. 390.

5. Cobden, *Three Panics, Political Writings*, p. 390.

6. Cobden, *Three Panics, Political Writings*, p. 390.

7. Quoted by Cobden, in *Three Panics, Political Writings*, p. 390.

8. *1793 and 1853 in Three Letters* [1853] in *Political Writings*, p. 201.

Sir Howard Douglas (1776–1861), an expert on gunnery and ship armor, was consulted by Sir Robert Peel in 1848 about introducing iron ships into the British Navy. James Nasmyth (1808–

1890) is best known as the inventor of the steam hammer. In 1840 he was visited by M. Schneider of Le Creusot who studied the obliging Nasmyth's sketches and then constructed the hammer in France. Passing through Le Creusot in 1842, Nasmyth was astonished to find his sketches made a reality by the enterprising French iron master. As the century progressed, Schneider, Krupp, and England's Armstrong-Vickers became Europe's triumvirate of armaments makers. *James Nasmyth, Engineer: An Autobiography*, ed. Samuel Smiles (New York: Harper [1883?]), pp. 246–250; William Manchester, *The Arms of Krupp, 1587–1968* (Boston: Little, Brown, 1968), p. 90.

The steam hammer proved indispensable in the forging of iron plate for warships and of the "immense wrought-iron ordnance" of Armstrong-Whitworth. "But for the steam-hammer," records Samuel Smiles, "indeed, it is doubtful whether such weapons could have been made." *Industrial Biography: Iron Workers and Tool Makers* (London: Murray, 1876), p. 289.

9. *1793 and 1853, Political Writings*, p. 201. Later, Shaw's Undershaft would agree: "The more destructive war becomes the more fascinating we find it." *Bernard Shaw's St. Joan, Major Barbara, Androcles and the Lion* (New York: Modern Library, 1941), p. 237.

10. *1793 and 1853, Political Writings*, p. 201.

Lord Collingwood (1750–1810), who took over Nelson's command after his death, was once reputed to be Nelson's peer as an admiral. Sir William Fairbairn (1789–1874), an engineer, invented a rivetting machine and patented wrought iron girders for bridges. George Stephenson (1781–1848) was an inventor and railway builder. He anticipated Sir Humphry Davy's miner's safety-lamp by three weeks in 1815, although posterity has regarded the Davy rather than the "Geordy" lamp as the first. With his steam locomotive, the "Rocket," Stephenson made the trial run on the Liverpool and Manchester railway in 1830, thus inaugurating the railway age. Samuel Smiles, *The Life of George Stephenson* (New York: Harper, 1868), pp. 187–188; 329–330.

116

Of the military consequences of Stephenson's achievement, J.F.C. Fuller has said, "It was George Stephenson more so than Napoleon or Clausewitz who was the father of the nation-in-arms." From the start Prussia grasped the strategic importance of railways by planning a system whereby, on the eve of war, troops could be speedily moved from the center of the nation to its borders. *The Conduct of War, 1789–1961: A Study of the Impact of the French, Industrial, and Russian Revolutions on War and Its Conduct* (New Brunswick, N.J.: Rutgers University Press, 1961), pp. 92–93.

11. *1793 and 1853, Political Writings*, p. 201.

12. *The Public Letters of the Right Hon. John Bright, M.P.*, ed. H.J. Leech (London: Sampson Low, 1885), p. 35. Ford Madox Ford, *No More Parades* (London: Duckworth, 1925), pp. 6–7.

In a semi-autobiographical anti-war novel, commended by Tolstoy as the *Uncle Tom's Cabin* of the late nineteenth century peace movement, the Austrian Bertha von Suttner's heroine tours the Bohemian battlefields of the Austro-Prussian war in 1866 searching for her husband. Her graphic record of the field after battle is intended as an appeal to humane feeling. *Lay Down Your Arms [Die Waffen nieder]: The Autobiography of Martha von Tilling* [1889], trans. T. Holmes (London: Longmans, 1892), pp. 252–262.

That emotional appeal is characteristic of the pacifist persuasion. Of a dozen well known books about the First World War only the pacifist Henri Barbusse's gives a prolonged account in *Under Fire* (1916) of what the variety of modern weapons can do to human bodies.

13. *Public Letters*, pp. 35–36. From a humanitarian impulse, Bright frequently spoke out against the carnage of war; but as one historian views his moral objections, Bright "...never used pacifist arguments. Indeed he was not a pacifist." Keeping his Quakerism separate from his politics, he supported both the suppression of the Indian Mutiny in 1857 and the side of the North in the American Civil War. A.J.P. Taylor, "John Bright and the Crimean War," *Bulletin of the John Rylands Library*, 36 (1954), 506.

14. Quoted in Taylor, "John Bright," p. 509.

15. Quoted in Ausubel, *John Bright*, p. 73.

16. *Public Letters*, p. 34.

17. *The Poetic and Dramatic Works of Alfred Lord Tennyson* (Boston: Houghton Mifflin, 1898), p. 205, *ll.* 366–374.

18. By the time of the Crimean War, the armaments manufacturers had already begun to supply arms on an international scale. The industry "...was so intimately bound up with the Crimean War that a certain poem should read:

> International cannon to right of them,
> International cannon to left of them,
> International cannon in front of them
> Volley'd and thunder'd."

H.C. Engelbrecht and F.C. Hanighen, *Merchants of Death* [1934] (Garden City, N.Y.: Garden City Pub. Co., 1937), p. 11.

19. Taylor, "John Bright," p. 522.

20. *Public Letters*, p. 216.

21. *Public Letters*, p. 217.

22. *Public Letters*, p. 217. And again succinctly to another correspondent in 1878: "To abolish tariffs is the only way which leads to the abolition of great armies." *Public Letters*, p. 208.

23. *Public Letters*, pp. 195–196.

24. *Public Letters*, pp. 272–273. William Morris had similar sentiments about bondholders and the Anglo-Egyptian dispute which he termed, "the Stockjobber's Egyptian War." *The Letters of William Morris to His Family and Friends*, ed. Philip Henderson (London: Longmans, 1950), p. 188.

25. *Public Letters*, p. 296.

26. Ausubel, *John Bright*, pp. 237–238.

Chapter Two

1. *The Crown of Wild Olive* [1866], in Vol. xviii of *The Works of John Ruskin*, ed. E.T. Cook and Alexander Wedderburn (London: G. Allen, 1903–1912), pp. 471–472.

2. *The Elements of Drawing* [1857], in *Works*, xv, 227.

3. *Modern Painters III* [1856], *Works*, v, 333–334.

4. Arthur Helps, *Conversations on War and General Culture* (London: Smith Elder, 1871), pp. 264–265.

5. Arthur Helps, "War," in *Friends in Council*, New Series, by Arthur Helps (London: John W. Parker, 1859), i, 88.

6. "War," *Friends in Council*, i, 99–100.

7. "War," *Friends in Council*, i, 131.

8. "War," *Friends in Council*, i, 119–120.

9. "War," *Friends in Council*, i, 118–119.

10. *Conversations on War*, pp. 272–273.

11. "War," *Friends in Council*, i, 116.

12. *Conversations on War*, p. 272.

13. *Conversations on War*, pp. 240–241.

14. *Conversations on War*, pp. 305–306.

Chapter Three

1. *The Crown of Wild Olive* [1866], in Vol. xviii of *The Works of John Ruskin*, ed. E.T. Cook and Alexander Wedderburn (London: G. Allen, 1903–1912), p. 460.

2. *Modern Painters III* [1856], *Works*, v, 410–411.

3. *Crown of Wild Olive*, *Works*, xviii, 459–460.

A poignant example of the callousness of the commercial spirit is found in Ford Madox Ford's account of the death of his grandfather, Ford Madox Brown. Madox Brown had spent twelve years painting frescoes in the Manchester Town Hall, after which the Lord Mayor and the Town Council passed a resolution to whitewash the frescoes and put over them advertisements of the products of the councillors and aldermen. "Thus perished Ford Madox Brown—for this resolution ... gave him his fatal attack of apoplexy. The bourgeoisie had triumphed." *Ancient Lights and Certain New Reflections; Being the Memories of a Young Man* (London: Chapman and Hall, 1911), p. 117.

4. *Crown of Wild Olive, Works,* xviii, 466.

5. *Crown of Wild Olive, Works,* xviii, 472.

6. *Sartor Resartus,* Bk. II, Ch. viii, quoted in *The Crown of Wild Olive, Works,* xviii, 468–469. By the First World War, Carlyle's Dumdrudge sentiment had become a commonplace. Shaw observed that the proposal that all soldiers go home and tend to their business since it was the ruling classes' war was nothing new: "...it was only a variation on the theme of Carlyle's well-known apologue of Dumdrudge." *What I Really Wrote About the War* (London: Constable, 1931), p. 272. The American Dalton Trumbo's *Johnny Got His Gun* written in the late thirties continues along this line, being a vehement denunciation of the ruling classes as the enemy.

7. *Crown of Wild Olive, Works,* xviii, 469–470.

8. It would be a mistake to discount the growing awareness of the working classes who were quite capable of coming to conclusions on their own, but if we were to assign the influence of prominent Victorian social thinkers upon each other and also upon working class thought, it would not be too far from the mark to note that Ruskin learned from Carlyle, Morris from Ruskin, and Shaw from the Socialist movement in which Morris was active.

9. *The Ethics of the Dust* [1866], *Works,* xviii, 368, note 6.

10. *Unto This Last* [1860], *Works,* xvii, 104 n.

11. *Fors Clavigera: Volume I* (1871), Letter 7, in *Works,* xxvii, 127.

12. *Unto This Last, Works,* xvii, 104 n.

13. *Munera Pulveris* [1862, 1863], *Works,* xvii, 141–142.

14. Quoted in *Munera Pulveris, Works,* xvii, 142.

15. *Munera Pulveris, Works,* xvii, 142.

16. *Sesame and Lilies* [1865], *Works,* xviii, 104.

17. *Munera Pulveris, Works,* xvii, 142.

18. *Unto This Last, Works,* xvii, 104 n.

19. *Munera Pulveris, Works,* xvii, 251–252.

20. *Time and Tyde, By Weare and Tyne* [1867], *Works,* xvii, 332.

Chapter Notes

21. *Munera Pulveris, Works,* XVII, 252, 251.
Ruskin calls attention to the distinction between the shield bearer and the "shield-seller." The shield bearer's or squire's ultimate duty is to die in battle without thought of material advantage. Governments should be cognizant of that duty when they venture to become "shield-sellers." *Fors Clavigera: Volume II* (1872), Letter 22, in *Works,* XXVII, 383. Aristophanes uses the term, "Shield-seller," in his play *Peace,* to describe the merchants of death of his time. Trygaeus, indignant over the never ending Peloponnesian War, proposes a toast: "And if any spear-maker, or retailer of shields, wishes for battles, in order that he may have a better sale, may he be taken by robbers, and eat barley only." *The Comedies of Aristophanes,* trans. W.J. Hickie (London: Bell and Daldy, 1872), I, 262.

22. *Munera Pulveris, Works,* XVII, 174–175.

23. *Munera Pulveris, Works,* XVII, 175.

24. *Munera Pulveris, Works,* XVII, 178.

Chapter Four

1. E.P. Thompson, *William Morris: Romantic to Revolutionary* (London: Lawrence and Wishart, 1955), pp. 240–249.

2. William Morris, *The Letters of William Morris to His Family and Friends,* ed. Philip Henderson (London: Longmans, 1950), pp. 80–83.

3. Quoted in Thomas Carlyle, *Memoirs of the Life and Writings of Thomas Carlyle,* ed. Richard H. Shepherd (London: Allen, 1881), II, 311.

4. Quoted in Thompson, *Morris,* p. 252.

5. Morris, *Letters,* Appendix II, p. 388.

6. Morris, *Letters,* Appendix II, pp. 388–389.

7. Morris, *Letters,* Appendix II, p. 389.

8. Quoted in Thompson, *Morris,* p. 246.

Chapter Five

1. Barbara W. Tuchman, *The Proud Tower: A Portrait of the World Before the War: 1890–1914* (New York: Macmillan, 1966), p. 229.
2. Tuchman, *Proud Tower*, pp. 229–230.
3. *The Letters of George Gissing to Eduard Bertz: 1887–1903*, ed. A.C. Young (London: Constable, 1961), pp. 251, 254–255; *George Gissing and H.G. Wells: Their Friendship and Correspondence*, ed. Royal A. Gettmann (London: Hart-Davis, 1961), p. 131.
4. J.F.C. Fuller, *The Conduct of War, 1789–1961: A Study of the Impact of the French, Industrial, and Russian Revolutions on War and Its Conduct* (New Brunswick, N.J.: Rutgers University Press, 1961), pp. 134–135.

The rapid developments in military technology fascinated Ford Madox Ford's Mr. Sorrell. Foremost among the modern fruits of industry which he would like to take back to the Middle Ages is the machine gun: "Above all, the machine gun." *Ladies Whose Bright Eyes: A Romance* (London: Constable, 1911), p. 10.
5. *The Crown of Life* (London: Methuen, 1899), p. 289.
6. T.W. MacCallum and Stephen Taylor, *The Nobel Prize Winners and the Nobel Foundation, 1901–1937* (Zürich: Central European Times Pub. Co., 1938), pp. 329, 338.

At the Hague Peace Conference in 1898, Count Munster of Berlin regarded Baroness von Suttner as working for Russia: "The Conference," he wrote home in disgust, "has brought here the political riffraff of the entire world, journalists of the worst type ... and female peace fanatics like Madame de Suttner, who yesterday again entertained the Russian delegation at a large banquet.... All this rabble ... are working in the open under the aegis of Russia." Quoted in Elie Halévy, *Imperialism and the Rise of Labour (1895–1905)*, Vol. V of *A History of the English People in the Nineteenth Century*, trans. E.I. Watkin (London: Benn, 1961), pp. 64–65.
7. *Lay Down Your Arms [Die Waffen nieder]: The Auto-*

Chapter Notes

biography of Martha von Tilling [1889], trans. T.E. Holmes (London: Longmans, 1892), pp. 47–48.

8. An anti-peace movement argument is worth noting here by way of contrast. Especially telling is the likeness pointed up between the operations of modern large industry and modern military strategy. Colonel F.N. Maude, who believed that "what Darwin accomplished for Biology generally Clausewitz did for the Life History of Nations nearly half a century before him," was the editor of the 1908 English edition of Clausewitz's *On War*. As a military man he was predictably reluctant to see nations give up military advantage, particularly that of surprise, which would be lost by a declaration of intentions. He seems to have been delighted by the irony of Andrew Carnegie working for world peace:

> Yet there are politicians in England so grossly ignorant of the German reading of the Napoleonic lessons that they expect that Nation to sacrifice the enormous advantage they have prepared by a whole century of self-sacrifice and practical patriotism by an appeal to a Court of Arbitration, and the further delays which must arise by going through the medieval formalities of recalling Ambassadors and exchanging ultimatums.
>
> Most of our present-day politicians have made their money in business — a "form of human competition greatly resembling War," to paraphrase Clausewitz. Did they, when in the throes of such competition, send formal notice to their rivals of their plans to get the better of them in commerce? Did Mr. Carnegie, the archpriest of Peace at any price, when he built up the Steel Trust, notify his competitors when and how he proposed to strike the blows which successively made him master of millions? Surely the Directors of a Great Nation may consider the interests of their shareholders — *i.e.*, the people they govern — as sufficiently serious not to be endangered by the deliberate sacrifice of the preponderant position of readiness which generations of self-devotion, patriotism and wise forethought have won for them?

"Introduction," *On War* [1832] by Karl von Clausewitz, trans. Col. J.J. Graham, ed. with introduction. Col. F.N. Maude. (1908; rpt. New York: Barnes & Noble, 1968), i, v, x.

9. George Orwell's observation during the Spanish Civil War typifies the usual contempt which the combatant holds for the jingo journalist who urges others to fight: "The people who write that kind of stuff never fight; possibly they believe that to write it is a substitute for fighting. It is the same in all wars; the soldiers do the fighting, the journalists do the shouting, and no true patriot ever gets near a front-line trench, except on the briefest of propaganda tours. Sometimes it is a comfort to me to think that the aeroplane is altering the conditions of war. Perhaps when the next great war comes, we may see that sight unprecedented in all history, a jingo with a bullet-hole in him." *Homage to Catalonia* [1938] (Boston: Beacon, 1955), p. 66.

10. "...[P]ropellants–it was the industry's way of speaking of the various kinds of powder," explains Lanny Budd's father to his son. The elder Budd was "head salesman of the Budd Gunmakers Corporation" in the first of Upton Sinclair's Lanny Budd novels which is in part an exposé of the private armaments industry's promotional activities just prior to the First World War. *World's End* (New York: Literary Guild, 1940), p. 32.

If we were to cast about for a model for Hannaford the inventor, it might be Hiram Maxim, although the parallel cannot be pressed very far. Maxim (1840–1916), who invented the automatic machine gun, formed the Maxim Gun Works in 1884. His gun was adopted by the British Army in 1889 and by the Navy in 1892. The gun works became part of Vickers in 1896. Calling himself a "chronic inventor" and having a variety of inventions to his credit, Maxim was very proud of his gun's superiority in the field to other similar weapons. Gissing might have read about Maxim's work in the newspapers just as readers of *The Crown* read about Hannaford's. One biographical detail that Maxim and Hannaford share is that they are both naturalized English citizens. That Hannaford was taken from life suggests itself because of details about him that call attention to themselves yet serve no functional purpose in the novel.

Chapter Notes

Chapter Six

1. Edmund Fuller, *George Bernard Shaw: Critic of Western Morale* (New York: Scribner's, 1950), p. 51.

2. V.G. Kiernan, *The Lords of Human Kind: Black Man, Yellow Man, and White Man in an Age of Empire* (Boston: Little, Brown, 1969), p. 223.

3. Bernard Shaw, *Bernard Shaw's Saint Joan, Major Barbara, Androcles and the Lion* (New York: Modern Library, 1941), p. 221.

4. With regard to calling out the troops, the military put down Communists for Schneider at Creusot in the 1880's; and soldiers massacred captured strikers at Krupp's Essen in 1921.

5. H.C. Engelbrecht and F.C. Hanighen, *Merchants of Death* [1934] (Garden City, N.Y.: Garden City Pub. Co., 1937), p. 108.

6. Engelbrecht, *Merchants of Death*, pp. 113–114.

7. From *Dreadnoughts and Dividends* (1914), quoted in Engelbrecht, *Merchants of Death*, p. 115.

8. William Manchester, *The Arms of Krupp, 1587–1968* (Boston: Little, Brown, 1968), pp. 236–237.

9. Jules Verne, *Twenty Thousand Leagues Under the Seas* (Philadelphia: Porter and Coates, n.d.), p. 71. It should be added that Schneider of Creusot forged the keel.

10. *Major Barbara*, p. 175.

11. George Bernard Shaw, *What I Really Wrote About the War* (London: Constable, 1931), p. 2.

12. Shaw, *What I Really Wrote*, p. 111.

13. Shaw, *What I Really Wrote*, p. 101.

14. Shaw, *What I Really Wrote*, p. 101. Ruskin had called that arrangement "practical" political economy.

15. Shaw, *What I Really Wrote*, p. 295.

16. Shaw, *What I Really Wrote*, p. 23.

17. Shaw, *What I Really Wrote*, p. 58.

Chapter Seven

1. George Bernard Shaw, *What I Really Wrote About the War* (London: Constable, 1931), p. 22.

Even a brief discussion of English war aims would be incomplete without a reference to Bertrand Russell's voice of protest against England's involvement. Russell wrote to the *Nation* for August 15, 1914, that England could not be absolved of her "share in the destruction of Germany." The most conspicuous group blamed for the start of the war were the "diplomatists" of all countries, whose national pride and lack of imagination allowed them to drift into war. In addition to this "set of official gentlemen," other forces were at work — including the munitions makers:

> And behind the diplomatists, dimly heard in the official documents, stand vast forces of national greed and national hatred — atavistic instincts, harmful to mankind at its present level, but transmitted from savage and half-animal ancestors, concentrated and directed by Governments and the Press, fostered by the upper class as a distraction from social discontent, artificially nourished by the sinister influence of the makers of armaments, encouraged by a whole foul literature of "glory," and by every text-book of history with which the minds of children are polluted.

The Autobiography of Bertrand Russell: 1914-1944 (Boston: Little, Brown, 1968), pp. 41-42.

2. Arnold Bennett, *Liberty: A Statement of the British Case* (London: Hodder and Stoughton, 1914), pp. 22-23.

The rumor that the Kaiser held large shares in Krupp's had been around Germany for some time. William Manchester regards the rumor as an "illusion" which persists even among modern historians. *The Arms of Krupp, 1587-1968* (Boston: Little, Brown, 1968), p. 208. The Krupps and the Kaiser were intimate in other ways, the Kaiser being godfather to Alfred and conferring the name Krupp upon Gustav von Bohlen when he married Bertha Krupp.

3. Shaw, *What I Really Wrote*, p. 2.

4. Bennett, *Liberty*, pp. 33–35.
5. Shaw, *What I Really Wrote*, p. 143.
6. Shaw, *What I Really Wrote*, p. 209.
7. H.G. Wells, *The War That Will End War* (London: Frank and Cecil Palmer, 1914), pp. 8–9. Hereafter referred to in the text as *End War*.

Chapter Eight

1. Robert Graves, who was nineteen years old when he began his war service for the duration, offers a physiological explanation for being affected by the war for a decade. After describing the sedative action of ductless glands upon "tortured nerves" as explained to him by a specialist in battle fatigue, he states that, "It has taken some ten years for my blood to run at all clean." He and Edmund Blunden talked about their state of hysteria at the end of the war, and "We agreed that we would not be right until we got all that talk on to paper." *Goodbye to All That: An Autobiography* (London: Cape, 1929), pp. 221, 361.

2. Frederic Manning, *Her Privates We* by Private 19022 (London: Davies, 1930), prefatory note.

3. Graves, *Goodbye*, pp. 188–189, 215–216, 240–241, 283–288.

Graves' battalion "...cared no more about the successes or reverses of our Allies than it did about the origins of the war. It never allowed itself to have any political feelings about the Germans," pp. 181–182.

4. R.C. Sherriff, *Journey's End* (New York: Brentano's, 1929). Edmund Blunden, *Undertones of War* (London: Cobden-Sanderson, 1928), p. 219.

A similar use of the name Krupp occurs in Manning's book when a corporal indicates his displeasure over excessive laughter in the trenches with the following ejaculation: "Laugh, you silly muckers! ... "You'll be laughing the other side o' your bloody

mouths when you 'ear all Krupp's blasted iron-foundry comin'
over!" *Privates*, p. 268.

5. Richard Aldington, *Death of a Hero* (London: Chatto
& Windus, 1929), pp. 277–278.

6. Erich Maria Remarque, *All Quiet on the Western Front*
[1929] (New York: Heritage Press, 1969), p. 210.

7. Siegfried Sassoon, *Memoirs of an Infantry Officer* [1930],
in *The Memoirs of George Sherston* (New York: Literary Guild,
1937), pp. 214–215.

8. Guy Chapman, *A Passionate Prodigality: Fragments of an
Autobiography* [1933] (New York: Holt, Rinehart and Winston,
1966), p. 281.

9. Chapman, *Prodigality*, pp. 138–139.

About the idealism of the recruit of 1914, C.E. Montague
writes, "It no more occurred to him at that time that he was the
prey of seventy-seven separate breeds of profiteers than it did that
presently he would be overrun by less figurative lice.... The early
volunteer in his blindness imagined that there was between all
Englishmen then that oneness of faith, love, and courage." *Disenchantment* (London: Chatto & Windus, 1922), p. 4.

Shortly before his death a week preceding the Armistice,
Wilfred Owen, who enlisted in 1915 and who was to become the
symbol of youth wasted on war, expressed his bitterness over
profiteering. After a period of convalescence for battle fatigue,
Owen went back to France in August, 1918. He had found the
home front difficult to endure, with "...the stinking Leeds and
Bradford war-profiteers now reading *John Bull* on Scarborough
Sands." Quoted in D.J. Enright, "The Literature of the First World
War," in *The Modern Age, Pelican Guide to English Literature, Volume 7*, ed. Boris Ford (Baltimore: Penguin Books, 1966), p. 166.

10. Rose Macaulay, *Potterism* (London: Collins, 1920), pp.
26, 36–37, 177.

11. Ford Madox Ford, *No More Parades* (London: Duckworth, 1925), pp. 6–7.

12. Montague, *Disenchantment*, pp. 186–188.

13. Arnold Zweig, *The Case of Sergeant Grischa* (New York: Viking, 1928); Jaroslav Hasek, *The Good Soldier Schweik* [1930] (Garden City, N.Y.: Sun Dial Press, 1937), p. 145.
14. Ernest Hemingway, *A Farewell to Arms* (New York: Scribner's, 1929), p. 53.
15. William L. Langer, "Two Score and Seven Years Ago: World War I in Retrospect," *Gas and Flame in World War I* [1919] (New York: Knopf, 1965), pp. xviii–xix.
16. Henri Barbusse, *Under Fire* [1916] (London: Dent, 1955), pp. 338–340.

Chapter Nine

1. A.J.P. Taylor, *English History: 1914–1945* (New York: Oxford, 1965), pp. 361–362.
2. Joyce Cary, *A Fearful Joy* (New York: Harper, 1949), p. 163.

In this novel Cary includes an example of the kind of protest some such people might have written. James Gollan, an industrialist who is Cary's idea of one of England's ministers of production in the First World War, receives the following letter: "It is men like you who are responsible for this fearful war and the deaths of a million young men. It is your muddleheaded greed and saber rattling which brought this destruction on us. The Germans only wished for peace. But our naval policy directly supported by you, by the steel and armaments manufacturers, made it impossible for them to trust us," p. 188.

3. The origin of the phrase goes back at least to the eve of the First World War. William Manchester records the use of it by Karl Liebknecht, leader of the German Social Democratic Party about 1914. Liebknecht objected to the "bloody international of the merchants of death" (*blutige internationale Händler des Todes*). *Arms of Krupp*, p. 260. The epithet "the bloody international" had some currency also.

4. Robert Graves and Alan Hodge, *The Long Week-end: A Social History of Great Britain, 1918–1939* (London: Faber, 1940), pp. 269–270.

5. Lawrence Dennis, "Beverley Nichols's Pacifist Manifesto," *Saturday Review of Literature*, 30 Sept. 1933, p. 142.

6. Beverley Nichols, *Cry Havoc!* (New York: Doubleday, 1933), pp. 3, 6. Published in England by Jonathan Cape in 1933.

7. Quoted in *Cry Havoc!*, p. 203. Sir Arthur Salter was a judge and later chairman of the railway and canal commission (1928). In 1922 he presided over the trial of Horatio Bottomley for fraudulent conversion, resulting in five years' imprisonment for the former war fund raiser and editor of *John Bull*.

8. Richard Hooker, *Yale Review*, n.s. xxxiv (1934), 168–171.

The tone of the other book reviewed, George Seldes' *Iron, Blood, and Profits: An Exposure of the World-Wide Munitions Racket* (Dodd Mead, 1934), is evident from its title. Seldes' belief is that "…no reason for war remains except sudden profit for the fifty men who run the munitions racket." The book is an example of the sort of overstatement that obscured the armaments industry's culpability in promoting war. Seldes charges the munitions makers with escalating armaments in 1906 by introducing the British "all-big-gun ship," *Dreadnought*, and again after the war by pointing out what pocket battleships might be made within the 10,000 ton limit set by the Washington Treaty of 1922.

9. H.C. Engelbrecht and F.C. Hanighen, *Merchants of Death: A Study of the International Armament Industry* (Garden City, N.Y.: Garden City Pub. Co., 1937), p. vii. Originally published by Dodd Mead in the United States and Routledge in England in 1934.

10. Quoted in Engelbrecht, *Merchants of Death*, p. 88.

Chapter Ten

1. Richard Hooker, *Yale Review*, n.s. xxiv (1934), 168;

TLS, 16 August 1934, p. 568; Philip Burnham, *Commonweal*, 11 May 1934, p. 55.

2. Graham Greene, *England Made Me* (London: Heinemann, 1935), p. 8. Krogh's fellow Swede, Alfred Nobel, said much the same thing when he wrote, "I am a citizen of the world; my Fatherland is wherever I work and I work everywhere." Quoted in *Merchants of Death*, p. 95.

3. Graham Greene, *The Confidential Agent* (London: Heinemann, 1939), pp. 81, 85.

4. Graham Greene, *A Gun for Sale* [1936] (London: Heinemann, 1961), pp. 24–25.

5. More than likely, Greene drew upon common knowledge about Sir Basil Zaharoff for his portrait of Sir Marcus. The two have in common extreme age, cosmopolitanism, a Greek origin, the taint of dishonesty arising from a legal action for theft in youth and even a fluff of white beard on the chin.

Zaharoff was born in 1849 of poor Greek parents in Anatolia. After moving to Odessa, his family Russianized its name. He entered the cloth trade with his uncle in Istanbul. Taking money from his uncle, he fled to England in 1873. He was tried and acquitted but it was later widely believed that he got his start with stolen money. From England he travelled to Athens where he went to work for the arms firm of Nordenfeldt, subsequently becoming an agent for Maxim. From dealing in arms, he was a millionaire by 1913 when he became a French citizen. Having done high level intelligence work for the Allies in the First World War, he was knighted by the British in 1918. He retired to Monte Carlo in 1926 and there had control of the casino.

Like Sir Marcus, there were gaps in his biography. He disappeared during the Turpin affair of 1889–90 when the English were accused of stealing the secret of a French explosive. Where was he? "Zaharoff's Boswells have been unable to find the answers to those questions.... If ever there was a Balzacian character it was Zaharoff—a financial adventurer beside whom Cesar Birroteau was a pigmy." Zaharoff died at the age of 87 on November 27,

1936, the year in which *A Gun for Sale* was published. Engelbrecht, *Merchants*, pp. 101, 105.

6. George Orwell, *Coming Up for Air* [1939] (New York: Harcourt, Brace, 1970), p. 20.

Bibliography of Works Cited

Aldington, Richard. *Death of a Hero.* London: Chatto & Windus, 1929.

[Anonymous.] Review of *Merchants of Death* by H.C. Engelbrecht and F.C. Hanighen. *Times Literary Supplement*, 16 Aug. 1934, p. 568.

Aristophanes. *Peace. The Comedies of Aristophanes.* Trans. W.J. Hickie. London: Bell and Daldy, 1872. I.

Ausubel, Herman. *John Bright, Victorian Reformer.* New York: John Wiley, 1966.

Barbusse, Henri. *Under Fire* [1916]. London: Dent, 1955.

Bennett, Arnold. *Liberty: A Statement of the British Case.* London: Hodder and Stoughton, 1914.

Blunden, Edmund. *Undertones of War.* London: Cobden-Sanderson, 1928.

Bright, John. *The Public Letters of the Right Hon. John Bright, M.P.* Ed. H.J. Leech. London: Sampson Low, 1885.

Burnham, Philip. Review of *Merchants of Death* by H.C. Engelbrecht and F.C. Hanighen. *Commonweal*, 11 May 1934, p. 55.

Carlyle, Thomas. *Memoirs of the Life and Writings of Thomas Carlyle.* 2 vols. Ed. Richard H. Shepherd. London: Allen, 1881.

Cary, Joyce. *A Fearful Joy.* New York: Harper, 1949.

Chapman, Guy. *A Passionate Prodigality: Fragments of an Autobiography* [1933]. New York: Holt, Rinehart & Winston, 1966.

Cobden, Richard. *1793 and 1853 in Three Letters* [1853]. *The Political Writings of Richard Cobden.* Ed. Sir Louis Mallet. London: Ridgeway, 1878.

————. *The Three Panics* [1862]. *The Political Writings of Richard Cobden*. Ed. Sir Louis Mallet. London: Ridgeway, 1878.

Dennis, Lawrence. "Beverley Nichols's Pacifist Manifesto." *Saturday Review of Literature*, 30 Sept. 1933, pp. 142–143.

Engelbrecht, H.C. and F.C. Hanighen. *Merchants of Death: A Study of the International Armament Industry* [1934]. Garden City, N.Y.: Garden City Publishing Co., 1937.

Enright, D.J. "The Literature of the First World War." *The Modern Age, Pelican Guide to English Literature, Volume 7.* Ed. Boris Ford. Baltimore: Penguin, 1966.

Ford, Ford Madox. *Ancient Lights and Certain New Reflections, Being the Memories of a Young Man.* London: Chapman and Hall, 1911.

————. *Ladies Whose Bright Eyes: A Romance.* London: Constable, 1911.

————. *No More Parades.* London: Duckworth, 1925.

Forster, E.M. *Two Cheers for Democracy.* New York: Harcourt Brace, 1951.

Fuller, Edmund. *George Bernard Shaw: Critic of Western Morale.* New York: Scribner's, 1950.

Fuller, J.F.C. *The Conduct of War, 1789–1961: A Study of the Impact of the French, Industrial, and Russian Revolutions on War and Its Conduct.* New Brunswick, N.J.: Rutgers University Press, 1961.

Gissing, George. *The Crown of Life.* London: Methuen, 1899.

————. *George Gissing and H.G. Wells: Their Friendship and Correspondence.* Ed. Royal A. Gettman. London: Hart-Davis, 1961.

————. *The Letters of George Gissing to Eduard Bertz: 1887–1903.* Ed. A.C. Young. London: Constable, 1961.

Graves, Robert. *Goodbye to All That: An Autobiography.* London: Cape, 1929.

————, and Alan Hodge. *The Long Week-end: A Social History of Great Britain, 1918–1939.* London: Faber, 1940.

Greene, Graham. *The Confidential Agent.* London: Heinemann, 1939.

————. *England Made Me.* London: Heinemann, 1935.

————. *A Gun for Sale* [1936]. London: Heinemann, 1961.

Halevy, Elie. *The Age of Peel and Cobden: A History of the English People, 1841–1852.* London: Benn, 1947.

————. *Imperialism and the Rise of Labour (1895–1905).* Vol. V of *A History of the English People in the Nineteenth Century.* Trans. E.I. Watkin. London: Benn, 1961.

Hasek, Jaroslav. *The Good Soldier Schweik* [1930]. Garden City, N.Y.: Sun Dial Press, 1937.

Helps, Arthur. *Conversations on War and General Culture.* London: Smith Elder, 1871.

————. *Friends in Council. New Series.* London: John W. Parker, 1859.

Hemingway, Ernest. *A Farewell to Arms.* New York: Scribner's 1929.

Hobson, J.A. *Richard Cobden: The International Man.* New York: Holt, 1919.

Hooker, Richard. "Peace, War, and Munitions." Review of *Merchants of Death* by H.C. Engelbrecht and F.C. Hanighen. *Yale Review* n.s. xxiv (1934), 168–171.

Kiernan, V.G. *The Lords of Human Kind: Black Man, Yellow Man, and White Man in an Age of Empire.* Boston: Little, Brown, 1969.

Langer, William L. *Gas and Flame in World War I* [1919]. New York: Knopf, 1965.

Macaulay, Rose. *Potterism.* London: Collins, 1920.

MacCallum, T.W., and Stephen Taylor. *The Nobel Prize Winners and the Nobel Foundation, 1901–1937.* Zürich: Central European Times Pub. Co., 1938.

Manchester, William. *The Arms of Krupp, 1587–1968.* Boston: Little, Brown, 1968.

Manning, Frederic. *Her Privates We* by Private 19022. London: Davies, 1930.

Maude, Col. F.N. "Introduction." *On War* [1832] by Karl von Clausewitz. Trans. Col. J.J. Graham. Ed. Col. F.N. Maude. 1908; rpt. New York: Barnes & Noble, 1968. I.

Montague, C.E. *Disenchantment*. London: Chatto & Windus, 1922.
_____. *Rough Justice*. London: Chatto & Windus, 1926.
Morris, William. *The Letters of William Morris to His Family and Friends*. Ed. Philip Henderson. London: Longmans, 1950.
_____. "Unjust War: To the Working Men of England" [1877]. *The Letters of William Morris to His Family and Friends*. Ed. Philip Henderson. London: Longmans, 1950. Appendix II.
Nasmyth, James. *James Nasmyth, Engineer: An Autobiography*. Ed. Samuel Smiles. New York: Harper [1883?].
Nichols, Beverley. *Cry Havoc!* New York: Doubleday, 1933.
Orwell, George. *Coming Up for Air* [1939]. New York: Harcourt, Brace, 1970.
_____. *Homage to Catalonia* [1938]. Boston: Beacon, 1955.
Remarque, Erich Maria. *All Quiet on the Western Front* [1929]. New York: Heritage Press, 1969.
Ruskin, John. *The Works of John Ruskin*. Ed. E.T. Cook and Alexander Wedderburn. 39 vols. London: G. Allen, 1903–1912. The following are titles and volumes in this edition:
    The Crown of Wild Olive [1866]. XVIII.
    The Elements of Drawing [1857]. XV.
    The Ethics of the Dust [1866]. XVIII.
    Fors Clavigera: Volume I [1871]. XXVII.
    Fors Clavigera: Volume II [1872]. XXVII.
    Modern Painters III [1856]. V.
    Munera Pulveris [1862, 1863]. XVII.
    Sesame and Lilies [1865]. XVIII.
    Time and Tyde, By Weare and Tyne [1867]. XVII.
    Unto This Last [1860]. XVII.
Russell, Bertrand. *The Autobiography of Bertrand Russell: 1914–1944*. Boston: Little, Brown, 1968.
Sassoon, Seigfried. *Memoirs of an Infantry Officer* [1930]. *The Memoirs of George Sherston*. New York: Literary Guild, 1937.
Shaw, Bernard. *Bernard Shaw's Saint Joan, Major Barbara, Androcles and the Lion*. New York: Modern Library, 1941.

Bibliography

_____. *What I Really Wrote About the War*. London: Constable, 1931.

Sherriff, R.C. *Journey's End*. New York: Brentano's, 1929.

Sinclair, Upton. *World's End*. New York: Literary Guild, 1940.

Smiles, Samuel. *Industrial Biography: Iron Workers and Tool Makers*. London: Murray, 1876.

_____. *The Life of George Stephenson*. New York: Harper, 1868.

Suttner, Bertha von. *Lay Down Your Arms [Die Waffen nieder]: The Autobiography of Martha von Tilling* [1889]. Trans. T.E. Holmes. London: Longmans, 1892.

Taylor, A.J.P. *English History: 1914–1945*. Oxford: Clarendon Press, 1965.

_____. "John Bright and the Crimean War." *Bulletin of the John Rylands Library*, 36 (1954), 501–522.

Tennyson, Alfred Lord. *The Poetic and Dramatic Works of Alfred Lord Tennyson*. Boston: Houghton Mifflin, 1898.

Thompson, E.P. *William Morris: Romantic to Revolutionary*. London: Lawrence and Wishart, 1955.

Tuchman, Barbara W. *The Proud Tower: A Portrait of the World Before the War, 1890–1914*. New York: Macmillan, 1966.

Verne, Jules. *Twenty Thousand Leagues Under the Seas*. Philadelphia: Porter and Coates, n.d.

Wells, H.G. *The War That Will End War*. London: Frank and Cecil Palmer, 1914.

Woodward, L. *The Age of Reform, 1815–1870*. 2nd ed. Oxford: Clarendon Press, 1962.

Zweig, Arnold. *The Case of Sergeant Grischa*. New York: Viking, 1928.

Index

Index

Industrialism 105
Instigators of war 4, 18-19, 39, 72, 79, 83, 84, 90; capitalists 4, 9, 14, 25, 30-31, 35, 38, 49, 51, 55, 71, 83, 88; heads of state 19, 36, 38, 49, 53, 71; munitions makers 4, 14, 49-50, 60, 61-62, 64, 83, 87-88, 89-91, 93, 94, 101-102, 103; overpopulation 70-71; press 40, 43-44, 49; wealthy class 37, 38, 53; weapons research 44-48
Internationalism in industry 49, 53, 74-75, 88, 90, 94-96, 100-101, 107-108
Invasionists 5, 6, 7, 20-21

Jingoism 37, 38, 40, 42, 49, 58, 81
John Brown (armaments firm) 53
John Bull (newspaper) 58
Journey's End (Sherriff) 69
Junkerdom 43, 53, 55, 56

"Kaffir Circus" 50
Kaiser 57-60, 63, 66, 67
Kaiserism 66
Kellogg Pact 91
Kraft, Maximillian *see* Craft, Maximillian
Krupp, Alfried 94
Krupp, Bertha 54
Krupp family: cannon makers 3, 92; cause of war 67; dispute with Vickers 90-91; fortunes of 65; characterization of 49, 50, 52, 54, 58-59; power of 50; relationship with the Kaiser 57-58, 60, 63-64, 66; reputation of 70
Krupp, Fritz 54
Kruppism 62, 63, 65-66, 114

Labor party 55-56
Langer, William L. 78-79

Lay Down Your Arms (Suttner) 22, 41-42
League of Nations 22, 88, 91
Long Weekend (Graves) 79

Macaulay, Rose, *Potterism* 75-76
Machine age 3, 7
Major Barbara (Shaw) 49-54, 67
Manchester, William 54
Manning, Frederic, *Her Privates We* 69, 71
"Maud" (Tennyson) 8, 11-13
Maxim, Hiram 90
Memoirs of an Infantry Officer (Sassoon) 69, 72-74, 82
Merchants of death 49, 53, 54, 84, 94, 101, 104, 105
Merchants of Death: A Study of the International Armament Industry 89-91, 92, 93
Michael Armstrong (Trollope) 3
Middle East 36
Militarism 39, 41, 58
Mitsui, Japan 88
Modern Painters (Ruskin) 17
Montague, C.E., *Disenchantment* 69, 76-77; *Rough Justice* 106
Morris, William 35-38
Munitions makers: attraction of 34; directors of 53; German 57-58, 61, 67, 89; importance to war 8; international dealings of 84, 91, 107; literature about 93-94; morality of 94, 105; prohibition of 62, 64, 65, 89; strength of 50-51, 59-60, 87-88 *see also under* Instigators of war

Nasmyth, James 7, 8
National priorities 2, 25, 32-34
Nicholas II, Czar of Russia 39
Nicholas, Beverley, *Cry Havoc!* 84-88

141

Index

War profiteering 19, 70, 71, 72–77, 79, 96, 98, 107 *see also* Instigators of war

Warrior class 26–27, 28, 42, 79

Wars: Afghan 15; Boer 49, 73, 87, 90; Chinese 15; Crimean 9, 10, 11, 13, 15, 26, 35, 49; Egyptian 15; Franco-Prussian 3; Revolution of 1848 5; World War I 1, 49, 55, 57–67, 69, 75, 80; World War II, 21, portents of 85–86, 87–88, 91–92, 112

War That Will End War (Wells) 59–67

Watkin, Absalom 9

Weapons control *see* Armaments limitations

Weapons research *see under* Instigators of war

Wells, H.G. 57, 84–85, 87, 114; *War That Will End War* 59–67

Working class 14–15, 27–28, 29, 38, 55

World War I 1, 49, 55, 57, 67, 69, 75, 80

World War II 21; portents of 85–86, 87–88, 91–92, 112

Zaharoff, Sir Basil 49, 101, 106

Zweig, Arnold, *Case of Sergeant Grischa* 77

143